A Seed of Hope Endorsement

A SEED of HOPE for a Journey Through Grief is a woman's memoir whose message of love, hope and determination toward dealing with grief--is a heartfelt symphony of personal and private moments collaged from a female narrative voice in time. Dr. Lynn Turner Smith is a childhood friend and was best friends with my younger sister, Teresa (now deceased). The telling of her journey from childrearing, adolescence through adulthood while growing up and rooted in Pineville, a small southeastern town in Bell County, KY after the death of her beloved mother is one that I remember like it was just yesterday. Lynn's *Mama* was a gentle, caring and socially astute pillar of our thriving town where folks sat on front porch swings and drank sweet pink lemonade while watching neighborhood children play.

A girly-girly lady of elegance, Ms. Dorothy (as she was lovingly called) seemed like the closest person to a saint from my perspective much like my own mother. Like mother like daughter, Lynn was part of a respected, educated, middle class and hardworking family that quietly broke color barriers in their professions during the Civil Rights Era of the 1960's without fanfare, protests or court cases. And, like Ms. Dorothy, Lynn has always cared about others sometimes more than she has cared for herself.

At 14 years old, after the death of her *Mama*, the author was thrust into the roles of caretaker, "woman of the house," and young family matriarch. As head-of-household, she answered without provocation to a younger sister Diane, her dad (Big Len), her grandmother (Shirley) and Aunt Addie (Dee Dee), yet she still excelled in school, became a cheerleader leader and high school peer leader. At such a young age, it is doubtful whether or not she clearly understood the extent of grief and loss associated with anyone as endearing as her beloved mother.

After the trajectory years have passed while writing, researching and coming to grips, face-to-face with such a major loss, Turner Smith's, *A SEED of HOPE,* serves as sacred and instructional text that translates how revelation, faith, prayer and hope are salve and salvation that can aid us toward spiritual growth in the depths of our souls-- where we often need healing the most.

Applying decades-long years of experience in social work, education and psychology with application in the academy and coupled with an affinity for African American literary voices such as Maya Angelou and biblical Scripture, Dr. Turner Smith, writes with an adult voice of measured analysis and reasoning. This author's literary life lesson offers a laying of healing "hands" rendered as would a transformative spiritual hymn that has been excerpted from the essence of her life.

I am hopeful that readers understand the difficulty evidenced in recording memory. The recollection of one's life stories in the autobiographical genre is often an arduous task that has the power to present a narrative worth reading, interpreting and understanding. Lynn Turner Smith's authentic story is a gift to the reader from the spirit of a healer and humanitarian who has spent an entire lifetime offering solace to others--her family, profession, church and community. While reading, *A SEED OF HOPE*, one has the promise of becoming spirit-lifted that translates to a Balm in Gilead, one that creates potential and opportunity to make life a beautiful place worth living again while grieving. If permitted, Dr. Turner Smith's testimony of hope through this literary text can serve as a guidepost on how to opt for faith while mending a broken heart in the face of this thing we call life--and the unexpected turns that impact the mind, body, heart and soul.

With gratitude, I am honored that Lynn has asked me to write this book commentary. She has always been one of my dearest home girls, friend - a sister in the spirit, colleague and now one of my favorite autobiographical authors of note. Our hometown of Pineville, Kentucky in the Appalachian Mountains congratulates her on a life honored in tribute from whence she came.
~*Mary E. Jefferson*
Child Advocate, Educator
The CERA Group—LLP, Louisville, KY

What Others Area Saying About A Seed of Hope

I highly recommend A SEED of HOPE for a Journey Through Grief to all who are seeking understanding about the Seasons of Life.
Dr. Lynn Smith, the author, has her finger on the pulse of life's experiences as she shares her journey, hoping that we can relate it to our journey. The various transitions through the seasons of her life are interesting, capturing the attention of her readers and uniquely leading them chapter-by-chapter as her journey unfolds, hoping to encourage others to never give in nor give up on life. The book expresses the need for faith in God if one is to succeed in life. When you pick up the book you can't put it down until you have finished. The writing and the flow of thoughts reflect Dr. Lynn Smith's spiritual maturity and scholarship gleaned from her doctoral studies. As her pastor and friend, I can validate much of the discussion highlighted in her book, for we shared many days watching God handle the questions in her life, heal a broken heart and bring her to a place of safety in her life. The book ought to give one a faith in Christ, it ought to refresh a faith in Christ, it ought to strengthen one's faith in Christ and give hope of life eternal because of one's faith in Christ. It's good reading. Well done, my friend, Dr. Lynn Smith for uniquely sharing your faith journey through grief.
~*Rev. Dr. T. H. Peoples, Jr.*
Pastor, Historic Pleasant Green Missionary Baptist Church, Lexington, KY

A Must Read for Anyone That Has Experienced the Loss of a Loved One
A SEED of HOPE is a riveting, heartfelt story that will resonant immediately with anyone that has experienced the loss of a loved one. We walk with Lynn on her extraordinary quest from an adolescent girl questioning her Mommas' God until she becomes a grandmother and finds acceptance. All the while holding a tenacious grip on her faith and the unconditional love of family. Rich with real-life and wisdom, this is a poignant story of strength, faith, and divine timing, as Lynn's Momma's God becomes her own.
~Charlotte Bowling Roth

Fertilized Seeds of Hope
Dr. Smith went deeply inside her psyche to extract not just memories but extremely painful feelings that ached once more in her soul. Readers should remain fully aware of what it cost her psychologically to recollect for our sake intimate family issues and sufferings. And yet…and yet…there is great healing in what she shared from her own experience. Healing that many people that have experienced the same or similar circumstances can relate to and hopefully allow the seed of hope that germinated in Dr. Smith to germinate in them as well. Each chapter of her book moves the reader from one level of healing to the next until the climax at the end. *A SEED* of HOPE, if read under the inspiration of the Holy Spirit, will inspire readers to renewed commitment in striving to endure. There are healing properties for the broken hearted contained in each chapter inspired by *A SEED of HOPE*.
~Rev. Herbert T. Owens, Jr.,
Assistant Pastor, Historic Pleasant Green Missionary Baptist Church

Faith in Times of Grief
A SEED of HOPE is an excellent account of Dr. Smith's journey in dealing with the loss of her mother, followed through the years by several close family members, including her father. I love how Dr. Smith is so real about her faith in God, yet sometimes struggling through the grief to allow God's love to cover and carry her. Its something we all deal with and her account of coming full-circle in her faith journey is such a blessing and comfort to others to also know that they, too, can survive the grief.
~Chrissy Luther

I'm Glad I Did
After the loss of many close family members. and the near loss of my husband I happened upon Lynn Smith's book and really wanted to read it. I'm glad I did. What I learned is that grief is a normal thing to grieve even in our Christian Faith (some say it isn't which is very sad), is God ordained and to not resist it. Embracing the loss helps us to heal when we take our feelings to Him and allow Him to heal us. God can use even the most tragic situations for our good.
~D. Stevens

Loss, Love and Inspiration

This book is wonderful. I cried, I smiled and I felt Lynn's emotions alive in my heart. A *SEED* of HOPE gripped me to keep turning the pages. It is a deeply personal story of love, struggles, and losses, yet finding God in tragedy. It is an open view into the depths of your soul concerning loss and God's love. There is also extra wisdom and inspiration in its words to use for daily living experiences.
~Candice Evans Peace

A Gifted and Generous Storyteller, a Candid Memoir

Dr. Lynn Smith generously shares her honest journey throughout the pages of her touching new memoir, *A SEED of HOPE.* She is a gifted and generous storyteller with tremendous insights and wisdom into the often arduous grief-process. Not a downer - filled to the brim with hope and positivity from her deep faith. Helped me navigate and process the recent passing of a family member in a healthy manner. A poignant testament wherein she vulnerably wades through raw grief, Lynn poetically sorts death and loss through the filter of healing, hope and deep faith. An intimate gift to readers who've lost loved ones; her prose is warm and familiar, as though spoken in person over coffee. A copy fell providentially into my hands at just the appointed time…helped prepare me for such a loss, coached me to give liberty to my grief and to drink the full cup.
~Mia White

Love, Loss and Growth

A *SEED of HOPE* is for anyone dealing with the loss of a loved one. It is a heartfelt personal journey that Dr. Lynn Smith shares with her readers. It is a story of loss, love and growth. It is wrapped with scripture and her own personal prayers. I feel that this book will help many others who are dealing with grief.
~Starla Jimenez

Grabs One at the Heart

There is something about *A SEED of HOPE* that grabs one at the heart. I think all of us as human beings can associate with the loss of a loved one at some stage in our lives, and how it affected our world from there onwards. Not only does *A SEED of HOPE* focus on loss, but it focuses on hope, something every human being searches for some time or another. I have found the book absolutely beautiful, encouraging, a worthwhile read and inspiring.
~Berdyne Styne

Authentic Hope-Filled Journey for Motherless Daughters

I loved this book. It's a beautiful raw account of the journey from grief to hope. I loved Dr. Smith's authenticity. Having lost my Mom when I was eleven there were so many parts of this story I connected with. It's so freeing to know that someone else has felt what you've felt and communicates it in such a real way. The way she writes really resonated with me. Dr. Smith speaks my language and I believe many motherless daughters will be blessed reading this book.
~Amazon Customer

A Seed of Hope
For a Journey Through Grief

Lynn Turner Smith, Ph.D., MSW

Soulful Life Design
Lexington, Kentucky

Published by Soulful Life Design Lexington, Kentucky 40514.

Cover design by R. Karim

ISBN 9780988770713
Printed in the United States of America

2nd Printing October 2016

DEDICATION

A *Seed of Hope* is dedicated first and foremost to God, my creator and the sustainer of my life. Secondly, *A Seed of Hope* is dedicated to all those who first knew and loved my sister and me.

Our Mother
Dorothy Lee Faulkner Turner
who taught us about God and left us with a lifetime of love and a legacy of faith.

Our Father
Lenuel Ray Turner

Our Paternal Grandmother
Shirley Beatrice Turner Moore

Our Maternal Grandmother
Sarah Faulkner

Our Great-Aunt
Addie Dewey Faulkner Towns

My mother-in-love, Stella Bessie Winkfield Smith; my Aunt Arnetta Winkfield Hill, and best friend, Teresa Diane Jefferson, who passed away before *A Seed of Hope* was finished.

FOREWARD

I am Diane Turner Johnson, sister of the author, Lynn Rae Smith. I was very excited to be offered the chance to write the foreward for her first book. However, when reality set in I was very terrified because I wanted it to be perfect. After thinking about it though, I decided I wanted it to be REAL and totally real is not perfect, so here it is.

Dr. Lynn Smith is the author of, *A Seed of Hope.* "Lynnie," as I called her when we were children (and I still do today) is a great sister. She is very bright, loving and has a very humble soul. She will illustrate in her first book how to work through the grief, fear, loneliness, guilt and even shame that many of us have struggled with at some point in our lives.

We lost our mother to cancer at the ages of 12 and 14 and as children lost part of our identity, but thank the Lord our mother, Dorothy, instilled hope (JESUS) in us.

In this book, my sister talks about the grieving process before our mother passed away, after she passed away and life today, because she believes it will help others. I truly agree. I look up to her because I truly see her as a great example of, "Stepping out on faith," no matter what. She is a fantastic wife, mother, grandmother, sister, friend and many other things I'm sure some of you can fill in. As the Director of *Soulful Life Design Coaching,* she believes in giving back what's been given to her in life . . . *Hope.*

Grief is a process and in case no one has ever told you - WE NEVER ARRIVE. It is one of those unspoken issues that no one is comfortable discussing. However, it is very important that we can openly speak about it in order to begin healing. It is ok to be sad, angry and confused. It's in those moments we will grow closer to the seed of Hope (Jesus).

~ Diane Turner Johnson

CONTENTS

Part III – Life Beyond Loss

HOPE...

Hebrew word tikvah, which originally meant to twist or weave, as strands of rope, making a tool capable of holding a heavy load securely; trustful expectation, the anticipation of a favorable outcome under God's guidance.
~ Holman's Bible Dictionary

At least there is hope for a tree: If it is cut down, it will sprout again, and its new shoots will not fail. Its roots may grow old in the ground and its stump die in the soil, yet at the scent of water it will bud and put forth shoots like a plant.
~ Job 14:7-9

NEVER LOOSE HOPE…

The butterfly is proof that beauty can emerge
from something completely falling apart.
~ Jane Lee Logan

Introduction

Life can only be understood backwards;
but it must be lived forwards.
~ Soren Kierkegaard

At the ages of 12 and 14, my sister and I experienced the loss of our mother, leaving us stunned and devastated. Hope Edelman in her book, *Letters from Motherless Daughters: Words of Courage, Grief and Healing*[1] sheds light on the complexities and challenges of losing a mother at such a young age. "After a mother's death, a daughter's painful road to healing begins. For some it is a lifelong struggle. Others may come to accept the loss as a catalyst for change as they try to move forward without leaving their mother's memory behind." *A Seed of Hope* is the story of a young girl's journey through grief.

Writer, Victoria Alexander,[2] believes the griever has three basic needs:

1. To find words for their loss
2. To say the words aloud
3. To know the words have been heard

A Seed of Hope details the complex journey my sister and I faced living in a motherless world. The book is part memoir, based mostly on the elusive and jagged memories of an adolescent, and part testimony as it traces my journey through accumulated losses to the arms of God.

Theologian, Walter Brueggemann's book, *The Message of the Psalms: A Theological Commentary,*[3] provides a framework for a journey through grief. He suggests that human beings regularly find themselves in one of three places in life: a place of orientation, disorientation, and new orientation. He describes orientation as: "A place in our lives where everything makes sense. It is a hope-filled place that evokes gratitude for the constancy of blessing, joy, delight, goodness, coherence and reliability on God." Psalms of trust fit within orientation as they express our trust in God's care and goodness.

Brueggemann reminds us that life does not stay orderly or coherent and there comes a time when our hope-filled place is, "Suddenly interrupted by a major life change, spiraling us into a place of disorientation, sinking us into a horrible pit, a broken place." Psalms of lament fit within this disorienting place and gives us words to express our deepest confusion and sorrow.

We all have experienced deep losses in our lives that spiraled us into a place of despair and hopelessness. Our natural reaction to such a major loss is the grief response – denial, bargaining, anger, depression and hopefully acceptance. Some losses, however, are so devastating that we delay or postpone grieving until we can face the magnitude of the loss. These disorienting losses can bring us to our knees and send us running to God.

Following our season of disorientation, we unexpectedly find ourselves in a place of grace, of rising hope and fresh possibilities. Brueggemann intimates, "The move to this place in our lives cannot be explained logically; it only arises from the goodness of God." This place of new orientation usually takes us by surprise, because after experiencing such a life-altering loss, we don't anticipate ever feeling whole again. " It is a place of new mercies where we suddenly understand what happened to us and who brought us up." Psalms of thanksgiving, wherein we thank God for what he has done for us, fit within this place of new orientation.

The Psalms and other scriptural promises from God to me are sprinkled throughout the book, corresponding to the seasons of human life and bringing speech to seasons of despair and joy. *A Seed of Hope* is filled with God's promises. The Psalms, in particular, helped me to find words to express my deepest sorrows as well as my most profound joys. They are especially helpful for the grieving process because they genuinely express both sides of the conversation of faith.

This book, like my life, is divided into three parts:

Part I – Life Before Loss, details the sacred ordinariness of life on The Hill with Momma and all those who first knew and loved me.

Part II – Life After Loss, describes the aftermath of being thrust into an unexpected place of loss and devastation in which all hope seemed lost.

Part III – Living Beyond Loss, describes coming full circle through accumulated losses to unexpected places of grace, rising hope and fresh possibilities for life.

Because grief is not an orderly, step-by-step process, this book is not written to fit neatly within the seasons of orientation, disorientation and new orientation. Grief is not a straight path from A to B. The journey through grief is more like movement through a spiral that winds and progresses from one dimension to another.

The journey through grief involves movement in all directions and in multiple dimensions. It is not the stages that are important, but the momentum.
~Elissa Bishop-Becker

According to Bishop-Becker,[4] grief is a continuous cycle of coming back to the same place, but experiencing it in a new way. Sometimes we move ahead only to discover we are back at an earlier stage. Even though we may arrive at a previous stage, we are not the same, nor is the intensity of the pain and sadness we feel. We may revisit the grief and sadness of one stage more than once until we can let go and move on. We must move through the process of reconciling what was lost and what is left. As we move through the grief spiral we become stronger as we allow God to transform our pain.

Writing my story took me back on a painful journey of remembrance, breaking my heart all over again. This is the story that the brave little girl within me wants to tell. It has taken 45 years for her to find her voice. It is her personal account of her grief journey and her struggle to find hope, peace, and healing. It is the story of her sorrow, her fears, her hopes and dreams. It traces important turning points in her life and provides clues as to how God was there all along shaping her for a future she could not see. It details her search for identity, purpose and meaning that could only be found by pursuing her Momma's God. It is only from this vantage point that she can see God's providence over her life. The emotional and psychological cost of bearing my soul was worth the heartbreak to the brave little girl. After a hundred starts and stops...this is her story. I write not only for her, but also for my little sister, and everyone who has ever had to say goodbye to someone they loved and needed.

We all have a story to tell, a core wound that only God can heal. This is my story. I hope my story intersects with yours and offers a glimpse of how God has been at work in your life too. I hope the seed of hope that germinated in me will germinate in you too.

Give sorrow words. The grief that does not speak
whispers the o'er-fraught heart, and bids it break.
~William Shakespeare, Macbeth, Act IV

PROLOGUE

December 3, 1971

"Kiss your momma goodbye," Daddy says to my sister and me.

I will never kiss Momma goodbye.
I will never tell her goodbye.

Being the obedient daughters Momma raised us to be, we both kissed her, but I vowed it was not goodbye.

Why did you let this happen God?
Where were you when I prayed to you?

Momma was the center of our universe. She was everything to us - our soft place in the world. My 14-year-old mind couldn't comprehend why God had taken her away from us. It was even more confusing for my sister, who was only 12 at the time. It was impossible to reconcile Momma's death against the backdrop of my childlike concept of God as the One who answers prayers. After all, that's what Momma said many, many times. She said, "You can pray to God about anything and He will answer."

Was Momma wrong? Was she mistaken?
Did my prayers not get through?
Is God hard of hearing?"

This experience prompted difficult questions a 14-year-old could not possibly answer or reason with. It would take years for me to integrate my childlike faith with who God really is and to answer the question: "Why would God leave two little girls confused and motherless?" Since Momma was gone, the only one left to answer my questions was Momma's God.

Part I
Life Before Loss

Before I formed you in the womb I knew you.
~ Jeremiah 1:5a

Our lives may be determined less by our childhood than by the way we have learned to imagine childhood.
~ James Hillman, The Soul's Code

CHAPTER 1
HOME

A song of ascents. I will lift up mine eyes unto the hills,
from whence cometh my help.
~ Psalm 121:1 (KJV)

I believe that one can never leave home.
I believe that one carries the shadows, the dreams,
the fears and dragons of home under the skin, at the
extreme corners of one's eyes and possibly in the gristle
of the earlobe. We carry accumulation of years in our bodies
and our faces, but generally our real selves, the children inside,
are still innocent and shy as magnolias.
~ Maya Angelou

I was born in the small town of Pineville in southeastern Kentucky, at the foot of Pine Mountain. My hometown is part of a legendary tale about a chained rock.

> High on the vaulted slopes of Pine Mountain,
> a large rock hangs over the town. In the
> 1930's the rock was allegedly harnessed by
> a large chain because children were having
> a hard time sleeping at night, afraid the rock
> would come tumbling down the mountain,
> and destroy the city.[5]

As a child, I sometimes dreamed of the chain coming loose and the rock tumbling down on us while we slept in our little five-room house. I always woke up in the nick of time, before the rock landed and destroyed us. Little did I know that the rocky hills I loved as a girl would indeed come crashing down.

I am no stranger to climbing hills. We grew up on Cypress Street, which we called, "The Hill." To get to our house, we had to climb two hills and then traverse about 14 wooden steps. Rather than climbing the steps one at a time, I would run them two-by-two. There was a perfectly good reason - snakes were plentiful and known to lurk beneath the steps.

I spent a lot of my childhood worrying about snakes and other unknown creatures that could possibly be waiting to get me. Some days I would completely avoid the steps and climb the hill beside them. I still remember scaling the steps, praying, *God, please don't let the snakes get me.* That's how I first came to believe that God answers our prayers. The snakes never got me. They came close. One day my little sister Diane and I were playing 'ring-around-the-rosy,' around the big tree in our yard. I suddenly became aware of something, looked down under my hand, and there was a black snake. Still, God protected me.

Our childhood home was nestled in the mountainside, surrounded by pear and apple trees and plentiful with dandelions. As a little girl, I loved picking yellow dandelions from our yard and taking them to Momma. After the dandelion flower turned brown and only seeds were left, I would close my eyes and make a wish. I believed the seeds had the power to make my hopes and dreams come true. I didn't know the floral meaning of the dandelion – that it is a gift to a loved one that will provide happiness and a promise of total faithfulness.

Diane and I were blessed to grow up in an extended family with Momma, Daddy and Aunt Addie, whom we affectionately called Dee Dee. She raised our mother, Dorothy, from a young age. Dee Dee's sister Sarah was not able to take care of her. We never knew why. Grandma Sarah lived in Ohio and we would often visit her and Momma's sister, Frances, during the summers. Our paternal grandmother, Shirley Bea, as everyone called her, lived across town on Breastwork Hill with our favorite Uncle Barton.

It is true what Pliny the Elder says about home: *"Home is where the heart is."* Although I left home many years ago, home is still in me, in every cell of my being. Memories of growing up in Pineville are more than sentimental. It was truly a beautiful beginning to life. Home was the place of orientation that Brueggemann describes in, *The Message of the Psalms,* a place of unconditional love and support. The beauty of the mountains could only be matched by the love that overshadowed us.

When I close my eyes and think about home, I can still smell the cypress, apple, and pear trees mixed with the mountain air. Everyone on The Hill was family. Life was simple. I remember running up and down The Hill, playing double-dutch, hopscotch, jacks, marbles, high waters, and hide-and-seek with sis, our cousins, and friends. I crowned myself the double-dutch queen of The Hill.

We learned everything that was needed for our life's journey on The Hill. We learned the true meaning of family – it's more than blood; rather, it's heart. Everyone looked out for each other. Although it was not a gated community, it was a protected one. There was no place you could go on The Hill without watchful eyes and the protective care of adults.

The Price's lived at the highest peak on The Hill. We could venture down The Hill to Aunt Georgia's, Anna's and our favorite cousin, Elsie's anytime. Diane and I were never without cousins or friends to play with. I always felt protected by our cousins Jackie, Hammer (Drake), Junior and Gwen who lived on the second level of The Hill. Austin and Jennifer would come later in life. All the kids would gather at Miss Joyce Whitley's house to play with

Linda, Lana, and their brothers and to eat some of Granny's famous cornbread. We would go down to the Tye's, Dyer's or Ferguson's who lived at the bottom of The Hill. Everyone loved it when our friend Curt, Jr. had his annual birthday party. Every kid in the neighborhood would be there.

Mrs. Cora and her two granddaughters, Paula and Cheryl, lived right below us. They looked like movie stars to us. Further down The Hill, my friend Shirley lived with her Aunt and Uncle – the Chapman's. We'd all meet up at the bottom of The Hill for the half-mile walk to school.

In the summers, The Hill was bustling with relatives and family friends that came to visit. Aunt Frances and her children would come from Ohio. Uncle Sonny, Momma's brother and cousins Ed, Sallie and Ruth and their children would also come to visit. The Hill was a place of beauty, a place of refuge. It was home.

CHAPTER 2
MOMMA NEM

*Yet you brought me out of the womb; you made me trust in you,
even at my mother's breast. From birth I was cast on you; from
my mother's womb you have been my God.*
~ Psalm 22: 9-10

*In the sheltered simplicity of the first days after a baby
is born, one sees again the magical closed circle, the miraculous
sense of two people existing only for each other.*
~ Anne Morrow Lindbergh

More than anything, The Hill was home because
Momma was there. Dorothy's love was the thread that held
the fabric of our family together; like a beautiful quilt. Her
presence and love were our nucleus; they held our family
together and maybe even held The Hill together. I have
never known anyone like Momma. She was the gentlest
and sweetest woman I have ever met. Diane and I were
privileged to grow up under her watchful and protective
wings. Wings we sometimes wished weren't so protective,
but would later grow to appreciate. She believed in us,
encouraged us and nurtured us. She affectionately called
us, "her girls." Nobody better ever mess with, "her girls."
She would say, "Momma loves you girls two tons."

Momma was beautiful to me. She had the most amazing
smile that would warm the hearts of all who she met. She
stood five feet and four inches tall, was medium build,

with beautiful brown skin and the prettiest legs. Momma wore her hair short with bangs and it was always styled beautifully with not a hair out of place. She wore pretty classic dresses which I can still remember. None of the women in our family wore anything but dresses.

Momma guarded us against the harshness of the world as long as she could. While our friends were outside playing long after the streetlights came on, you could find Diane and me perched in the window watching them play. We were well into our teens before we played outside at night. We would find out later that hide-and-seek is much more fun in the dark. We always felt like we were being deprived of a normal childhood, only to find out later in life that Momma shielded us as long as she could.

Dorothy was smart, kind and compassionate. To this day, I still hear stories about how much people admired and loved her. She was the model Proverbs 31 woman. A strong woman of faith; she showed us how to live and how we should treat people that we encountered in life. Aunt Frances, Momma's sister, maintains, "Dorothy, was too good for this world." I remember one particular day Momma overheard us making fun of a girl at school and she stopped us in our tracks. She said, "Always treat people the way you want to be treated. Always treat everyone with kindness." Momma's kindness may have been mistaken for weakness, but she wasn't weak. She had a quiet strength about her. My cousin Drake recently shared a story about Momma breaking up a fight between two young men at the annual church picnic. He said, "Your Momma got between them and said, 'No! Not here!' and they stopped fighting, which was surprising."

Momma was funny and afraid of every living and moving creature or critter, large or small. My cousins from Ohio got a kick out of teasing her with rubber spiders and snakes just to watch her run screaming out the door. Aunt Frances could be heard raising her voice saying, "Leave my sister alone!" Momma definitely passed her fears of real and imagined creatures on to me.

Momma was a hairdresser when we were younger. I still remember the smell of the straightening comb and curlers heating on the gas burner of our stove, mixed with the scent of Royal Crown and Ultra Sheen hair grease. Almost every woman in the community made their way to our little kitchen to get their hair done. Diane and I would always look forward to the ladies coming to the house because they would slip a nickel, and sometimes even a quarter, into our hands before leaving. I loved to hide in the living room and listen to their conversations, mostly about God and raising children. I loved to hear Momma laughing as she was straightening and curling the ladies hair.

Momma loved to read and passed her passion for learning on to us. She could always be found drinking a Coke, smoking a cigarette, and reading some kind of book. She made sure we were surrounded by books of every kind - all the children's fairytales, encyclopedias, enrichment books, and even a ten-volume set of the *Children's Bible Story*. Momma's favorite book to read was the Bible. She would read to us and make biblical characters come alive. I was born a dreamer so it wasn't hard for me to believe in fairytales and happily ever after. I loved to sit under Momma's arm – me on one side and Diane on the other, as she read to us. We would beg her to read one more story and she happily did. Momma taught us to read and write long before we went to school. She would tell Diane and me how smart we were. She would say, "Momma's pretty girls are so smart." But she reminded us on many occasions, "Pretty is as pretty does."

One of my most favorite memories of Momma, though, is sitting between her legs on the floor as she braided my hair. I hated getting the tangles brushed out, but there was just something about Momma's hands in my hair. Lonnae O'Neal Parker, in her Washington Post article entitled *Balm*,[6] writes, "The bonding that happens between a mother and daughter through hair is one of the strongest generational bonds. By attending to her daughters' hair each morning, a mother is attending to something deeper than a beauty ritual." I had not thought about hair braiding as a magical and sacred bond between a mother and a daughter. I still remember and miss the touch of Momma's hands in my hair, but mostly I remember how she made me feel. It was our time – just the two of us.

Many memories of Momma have faded away. I sometimes frantically search through the few tattered pictures that remain for clues about Momma and our life with her. In almost every picture, Diane and I are adorned in pretty dresses, white socks with ruffles, and patent leather shoes. I still remember those itchy, 'can-can slips.' Momma's best friend, Mrs. Inez Bishop, would load us up in her green station wagon and take us shopping with her daughters, Jan and Sissy. We would spend the day in Middlesboro. On Easter Sunday, we would all have on frilly dresses, hats (which my sis absolutely hated), gloves and a purse to match our shoes. Momma took great pains to ensure that she sent her girls into the world, making it clear we were valued and loved. It is because of Momma that I still love beautiful dresses and yes, even black patent leather shoes.

Momma was a Godly woman. She taught us about God and Jesus by example. Before she tucked us in at night she would kneel next to us to pray:

Now I lay me down to sleep,
I pray the Lord my soul to keep.
If I should die before I wake,
I pray the Lord my soul to take.

We would end the prayer by asking God to bless everyone in our family, name by name. Momma would wait patiently until we finished praying for everyone we could think of. Every Sunday she would take us to Sunday school and church and prayer service on Tuesdays. There was never a question as to whether or not we were going to church. Diane and I sometimes accompanied Momma to the women's missionary meeting at Mrs. Crockett's house down The Hill. I still, lovingly, remember those hard oatmeal cookies she served.

Momma loved to play the piano and taught us to play as well. Later she arranged for us to take piano lessons from Mrs. Wilson who lived near the school. I hated going to Mrs. Wilson's because I wanted Momma to teach me to play. Momma was much more lenient and loving than Mrs. Wilson. It would be many years later that I would discover, in the brief time Momma was with us, that she taught us everything we needed for life. She instilled in us values for life. She taught us how to love unconditionally and how to treat people with kindness and respect. She taught us the importance of family.

Miss Dorothy, as everyone called Momma was affectionate, always with plenty of hugs and kisses to go around. Mrs. Cora, who lived below us, often said, "Here comes the kissing Turner's," which was a tribute to Momma and her love. Momma's love was strong and steady; she was the buffer between us and the world, a bottomless well of affection. As much as she loved Diane and me, she had plenty of love to go around for everyone, especially for her husband, our Dad, Lenuel Ray, whom she loved unconditionally.

I was named after Daddy. Everyone called him, Big Len, and me, Lynnie Rae. Daddy stood six feet and three inches tall. He was a tall, dark and handsome man – definitely a ladies' man, which proved to be a point of contention between him and Momma. Daddy was quiet, introverted, a gentle man; a tower of strength from his days of being a Marine. He lived a simple life. He never owned a car, preferring to walk everywhere. As a little girl, I remember Daddy holding our hands as we walked down The Hill, and we would almost have to skip to keep up with his giant steps. He was the first man I ever loved. He was our hero.

Daddy was a man of few words. It would take him forever to answer a question or to express what was on his mind. He grew up with his stepfather, Jeff T. Moore, Granny's husband. Dad was only eight years old when he died. Although he didn't grow up with his biological father in the home he became close to his sister, Louise, who lived in Dayton, Ohio. I now wonder how experiencing death at such an early age impacted him, his outlook on life and how he presented himself in the world.

Daddy was a basketball star during his high school years at Roland Hayes. After high school he went off to the Marine's when he was only 17 and fought in the Korean Conflict. I recently found letters my grandmother had written to him when he was overseas. She said: "Son, I tried to tell you not to join the service, but the good Lord will watch over you." Whatever he saw and experienced in the war impacted him tremendously in life.

There were some things about Daddy that we didn't know about or understand when we were younger. When we were a little older, Momma introduced Diane and me to Dad's son Charles, who lived in Louisville. We were never told the circumstances of his birth. We were just told, "this is your older brother." He even came to live with us for a while.

Daddy taught us a strong work ethic by example. He worked as an orderly at Pineville Hospital. I remember thinking he was a doctor when I was young. He would leave the house dressed in his crisp, starched white uniform, white socks and white shoes. Whenever we had a boo-boo or became sick, it was Daddy that would render first aid and give us medicine. When my sister fell and broke her arm, Daddy put the cast on her arm. That was one of his duties at the hospital. He was the one who took us to the dentist, and even though I was terrified, Daddy's presence made me brave. In the evenings, he cleaned the Pineville Health Department. Sometimes he would take us with him to clean, but more often he would take our cousin, Drake, who still credits Daddy with teaching him how to work.

Growing up with Daddy in the house was reassuring. It provided a sense of safety and security for us. He was our protector. As little girls we would anxiously wait for him to get home from work, sometimes hiding from him. Daddy rarely got angry or raised his voice. His discipline of us involved him giving us a stern look. Sometimes he would threaten us with his belt, but he never used it.

I didn't know much about Daddy's faith when I was young. He didn't talk about his beliefs. He sang in a male chorus with Charles Zachery and others. In those days, children were taught not to ask questions, nor to meddle in grown folks' conversations or business. I was quite inquisitive and perceptive as a little girl, but learned early in life to keep what I knew to myself. I overheard things I wish I had never heard, but I never asked anyone about them.

I was only two years old when my little sister, Diane, was born and I don't remember much, except my excitement when Momma and Daddy brought her home. She had big brown eyes and a smile that lit up the room. She was so cute, like my very own doll to play with. As we grew up together on The Hill, we became comrades. Once I started school, I would fake a stomachache so that I could stay home and play with her. We did everything together. We played together and got in trouble, her much more than me. Momma would dress us in matching dresses and outfits - which was cute when were young, not so much so when we got older. Diane was so much fun to be around. I was always so serious, even as a child. She was shy but brave; curious and a little mischievous. We spent our days playing with Barbie dolls, jacks, paper dolls, puzzles and board games. We were never bored with each other. To this day, I consider her the strongest and bravest person I have ever known.

Christmastime was my favorite time as a little girl. It was big in our house. Diane and I would search for our gifts on Christmas Eve. One year we each decided to open one gift. When we wrapped them back up, we accidently switched the boxes and were caught on Christmas Day. I loved Christmas, not only because of the many gifts we received, and there were many. I loved the time we spent together as a family. I loved decorating the tree with sis and Momma, cooking Christmas dinner in the kitchen with her and Dee Dee, and baking desserts with Granny. Generational bonds were being made as we were taught about life and how to put in a pinch of this and a dab of that to make something delicious. It was during this time that I learned to make macaroni and cheese, dressing, homemade rolls and other dishes that are part of our family recipes that were made with love. To this day, I try to replicate the feeling that we had in our house on Christmas morning.

We would visit Granny and Uncle Barton on Breastwork Hill often. The Turner side of the family planted their roots on that side of town. Uncle Bill, Granny's brother, a preacher, lived next door to her. Uncle Charles, Aunt Elizabeth and our cousins, Gene, Franklin, Donald, Eddie and Shirley lived at the bottom of the hill. I loved visiting Aunt Elizabeth, she was always so sweet. In the summers Granny's sisters, Roberta, Pauline and Maxine would come to visit with their children. We always loved when Maria and Susan came. Diane and I are granddaughters and great nieces of coal miners who died before we were born. Granny's husband, Jeff Thomas Moore, was described as a man of faith. He was a coal miner who died from black lung when Granny was only twenty-four.

Granny's little four-room house did not have indoor plumbing and I can still remember those dreaded trips to the outhouse and that awful smell. On tippy toes, I would barely sit my bottom on the wooden seat that was lined with newspaper for fear that a snake would crawl up and bite me. The goal was to use the toilet and get out as quickly as possible.

Granny was a fair-skinned woman with straight, silky black hair. She was sometimes mistaken for being white.

We were told that her mother, Hattie, was Indian. Granny always wore floral housedresses with pockets and house shoes. She was a kind and generous woman. I loved going to her house because love lived there. It was a safe haven. The saying is true: *A garden of love grows in a Grandmother's heart.* I know it is true because of Granny's heart. She would always welcome us with a big hug and homemade cookies. Sometimes Diane and I would spend the night with her. I remember Granny giving us a bath in her large tin tub; after bath, I'd crawl into bed next to her, snuggling up as close as I could get. It felt so comforting next to her. Like nothing in the world could harm me.

My favorite memory of Granny was baking with her. We would bake homemade biscuits, cookies, candy and cakes. To this day, I still cannot master Granny's fluffy biscuits. I believe it was the love in her hands that made them so fluffy. She would make the best homemade pound cake with caramel icing I have ever tasted.

Granny had a heart condition – an enlarged heart, which kept her from participating fully in life. I believe her heart was enlarged because it was overflowing with too much love or maybe because it had been broken by the death of her husband. She had too many heart attacks to keep count, like the cat with nine lives. She would go into the hospital and after a few days, come back home. Each time she went in, we thought she wouldn't make it back. I remember praying, *God please bring Granny back home to us*, and He always did. Even though she did not always feel up to going to church, Granny never missed playing bluegrass gospel music on the radio every Sunday and listening to the sermon. I believe she was a walking sermon, an example of God's grace.

Our Aunt Dee Dee was more like a grandmother to us than an aunt. Her life revolved around Momma whom she raised from a young girl. She was about five feet tall with brown skin. She always wore her hair pulled up in a bun. Dee Dee, with only a sixth-grade education, was conscientious and strong; the no-nonsense one in the family. She wasn't able to complete school because she had to work to support her family. Dee Dee was a devout Christian woman and lived her life as such. Her spirit and faith seemed indomitable. I believe she got her strength from overcoming many harsh realities in life.

Dee Dee was widowed at the age of forty-five. Her husband, Uncle Albert "Bud" Towns, survived two coal-mining accidents. In the first mining accident at Kettle Island, he was buried alive, then rescued. In the second explosion at Four Mile in 1945, Uncle Bud took charge and is credited with leading nine miners to safety until they were rescued. The miners said, "Bud Towns collected and rationed the food and water but wouldn't take any for himself and made us lay down together for warmth." In the dark, afraid, the rescued miners said, "Bud Towns prayed, quoted the scriptures – The Psalms – and preached a sermon on faith to them. He kept them sane until they were rescued." [7] Maybe that's where my love for the Psalms came from.

After being trapped for days and then rescued, the nine miners were taken to Pineville Hospital to the men's ward. It is told that the men were nearly dead from hypothermia, dehydration and respiratory failure. In 1945, the hospital was still segregated. Someone discovered that Bud Towns, the only black miner, had been placed in the 'white ward' with his fellow miners and a gurney was brought in to move him to the 'colored ward.' All the miners rose up with hoarse shouts saying: "Leave Bud alone. Leave him there where we can see him. He was the best man there." The Pineville Hospital was integrated from that time forth because of the heroic acts of Uncle Bud. He died three months later, at the age of 52, from bronchial pneumonia and carbon monoxide poisoning. His legacy of faith and hope has been passed down through our family's generations.

Dee Dee was always part of our lives. Daddy moved in with Dee Dee and Momma after they were married. My favorite memory of Dee Dee is sitting on her lap in her rocking chair. Diane and I would run to her lap when we got in trouble or when we just needed her comfort and love. When in trouble we would go running to her, crying: "Help me Dee Dee," as if she could save us.

Dee Dee worked hard all her life as a maid to a local attorney and his wife. She would leave for work at 7:00 in the morning with an apron wrapped around her dress. She cooked, cleaned and hosted parties for the family until she was 75 years of age. She still only made $75 per week when she retired. Without the social security and black lung checks she drew from Uncle Bud, she would not have been able to survive. Sis and I would often stop by and visit her while she worked. It was customary for us to go to the back door to see her. When I became a teenager, I would go the front door and ring the doorbell, vowing to never go to the back door again. The attorney's wife would answer the door and say, "Addie, Lynnie is here." She never once said, "You need to go to the back door," although I could sense she wasn't too pleased.

Dee Dee was serious about serving the Lord. Diane and I both experienced her washing our mouths out with soap on several occasions for saying bad words or things 'unbecoming of a young lady.' Things like, fart, lie and hell. Who knows what would have happened if we had really said a bad word. We would witness her raising her hands to praise the Lord at church and prayer meeting, and wonder what in the world was wrong with her. She believed in keeping the Sabbath holy. We weren't allowed to play cards on Sunday and could not go to the movies with our friends. Dee Dee and Momma always cooked Sunday dinner on Saturday so there wouldn't be anything on Sunday but church. We always thought she was too old fashioned. It wouldn't be until later in life that we understood she was teaching us how to live a faithful Christian life. We were blessed to grow up under the nurture and care of these strong men and woman who had faith in God. Their seeds of faith would nurture Diane and me and future generations.

CHAPTER 3
BETHEL

For in this hope we were saved. But hope that is seen is no hope at all. Who hopes for what they already have?
~ Romans 8:24

The ache for home lives in all of us. The safe place where we can go as we are and not be questioned.
~ Maya Angelou

Bethel Baptist Church was an extension of our home. Bethel is defined in the Bible Dictionary[8] as "a hallowed or holy place, a chapel for seafarers." It was the place that my childlike faith was rooted and nurtured. As children, we would walk to Bethel with Momma and Dee Dee, about one mile from our house on The Hill. Our family never owned a car, which wasn't uncommon, since many blacks in the community did not. We walked most places unless someone stopped to give us a ride. Mrs. Inez, Momma's friend would often pick us up. At church we would meet up with all our cousins and friends who lived in Straight Creek, Wallsend, and Cumberland Avenue.

Bethel was the place I accepted Jesus as my Lord and Savior. I came to believe the words to the song we sang often, *Jesus Loves Me*. At the age of nine, I confessed a hope in Christ and was baptized in the lake near the entrance of Pine Mountain State Park because Bethel did not have a baptismal pool. I can still remember Reverend Brooks in his white robe and booming voice, singing:

Wade in the water
Wade in the water, children
Wade in the water
God's gonna trouble the water

Reverend Brooks stirred the water with a big stick as he took me by my hand to baptize several others and me on that day. I can still remember the feeling that came over me. A feeling I could not explain then, but now recognize as the touch of God's Spirit. I remember singing in the Junior Choir with my friends and cousins, songs like, *We Have Come This Far by Faith* and *Just a Closer Walk With Thee.* In the summers we all attended Vacation Bible School together and the annual church picnic.

Momma was the church pianist and church clerk. She had a beautiful voice and would sing her favorite song, *Up Above My Head.* Reverend Brooks taught us the books of the Bible through song, and his wife, Mrs. Brooks, taught our Sunday School class. Sometimes, when I can't remember where a particular chapter in the Bible is located, I inadvertently start to sing the books of the Bible to locate the book I am searching for.

After Sunday school, the kids would rush across the street to Mr. Parrot's Grocery Store that was attached to his house. It couldn't have been any bigger than 10 x 10 feet, but we would all crowd in the store to purchase our candy. Before church started we would gather on the last two pews, armed with our treats. When we got too loud, which was often, an adult would turn around and tell us to hush. Diane and I would avoid eye contact with Momma on the piano when we got too loud. On a couple of occasions, she stopped playing the piano, came to the back of the church and marched us to the front pew to sit right in front of her. Little did we know that the songs, scriptures and sermons we barely listened to about God and Jesus were seeping into our hearts and souls. To this day, I know almost every gospel song and hymn by heart.

Bethel became so precious to me, particularly in later years as I discovered how much she had given me. The people in Bethel will always hold a special place in my heart and in my life, and the memories grow more precious as the years pass. A few years ago, my husband, Michael was called into the ministry; he was then invited to preach at Bethel for Homecoming Day. It was truly a homecoming for me. I was moved and filled with gratitude to be back in my home church where I first became acquainted with my Lord and Savior and where I first experienced the love of his people.

CHAPTER 4
THE UNCHAINED ROCK

In peace I will lie down and sleep, for you alone,
LORD, make me dwell in safety.
~ Psalm 4:8

The violets in the mountain have broken the rock.
~ Tennessee Williams

1967

Life on The Hill was good. We had everything we needed – family, friends, and love. Why is it that when life is going great, something inevitably happens to upset everything? When I was 10 years old and Diane was 8, my childhood nightmare about the chained rock coming loose, came true. It wasn't the legendary chained rock at Pine Mountain that was loosed, but a large boulder rolled down the mountain, crashing into our kitchen, destroying our home and displacing our family. I sometimes think it was a forewarning of the trouble that would come later to our family. By the grace of God, no one was home at the time. I remember telling God, *Thank you for keeping our family safe.*

We temporarily moved off The Hill that we loved into public housing until we found a permanent home. I hoped and prayed that we would move back to The Hill, but we didn't. That summer, Diane and I went to visit Aunt Frances and Grandma Sarah for two weeks in Washington Court House, Ohio. We often visited them with Momma in the summers. This was the first time we had gone to Ohio without Momma.

Grandma Sarah was strong, sweet and funny. She was a stout woman who was about four feet tall and some inches. She dipped snuff and watched her television shows most of the day. She would say, "Honey, it is good to see you, I'll see you later. You better go before it gets dark." This meant she was ready to get back to her television shows, since it was still daylight.

Aunt Frances was at the same time tough and tender. She was always so kind to Diane and me. Aunt Frances and Uncle Raymond had eight children. We would go with Uncle Raymond to his shoe shop in Columbus. He was the first person I'd known in our family to own a business. I vowed that I, too, would own a business someday.

While we were in Ohio, Momma, Daddy and Dee Dee moved us into a huge green two-story house with three bedrooms and a big back yard on Maple Street. It was our dream house. Every room had a fireplace and as soon as Diane and I walked through the door, we ran up the twelve stairs to see our room, where we found twin beds adorned with pink and white bedspreads with ruffles. Our bedroom was next to Momma and Daddy's and Dee Dee's was downstairs. We were all back together again. We were home. But I still missed life on The Hill with my friends and cousins.

Life on Maple Street was still segregated, with whites living on one side and blacks on the other. We had a new set of neighbors that became like family, just like on The Hill. The Dye's and Cornett's lived directly across the street from us. Jessie and Jack Mays and their children lived next door. We could venture behind us to Cumberland Avenue where the Cloud's, Lugo's, Jefferson's, Zachery's, Bishop's, Hill's and many more families lived. A year or so later, Granny moved from Breastwork Hill right next to us in a little white house. That year I learned that even though bad things may happen to us in life, God can and does work them out for good. The boulder may have wrecked our house, but our family remained intact.

We settled into our new home and life on Maple Street. Momma went to business school and was hired by the local welfare office as a clerk. Momma was the first black to be hired there. My friend Retha recently shared that she always admired the way Momma always dressed professionally. Diane and I would go by her office to visit her sometimes after school. Everyone at her office loved her and told us how much. Momma got off work at 4:30 every day and I would walk to the corner to meet her. And sometimes we would sit on the front porch swing after she got off work and we would just swing and talk.

Every morning I would meet my friends, Retha, Teresa and the Bishop and Cloud girls at the corner of Maple for our walk to school. On our way, we would make a pit stop at the donut shop, and after school, the ice cream shop. It was a normal teenage life – school, ball games, cheerleading, pimples, boys, church and hanging out with friends. Yes, life was good on Maple Street.

CHAPTER 5
THE VALLEY

*A psalm of David. I call to you, LORD, come quickly to me;
hear me when I call to you.*
~ Psalm 141:1

*Because life does not stay orderly or coherent, our
hope-filled season is suddenly interrupted by a major life change,
spiraling us into a place of disorientation.*
~ *Brueggeman, Praying the Psalms*

October 1971

That fall, the sacred ordinariness of life was upset when
Momma got sick and had to go to the hospital. I remember
her having a terrible cough that would not go away. We
came home from school one day to learn that Momma
would have to go to Knoxville Hospital for surgery. No one
told us what was wrong with her. No one mentioned the
word "cancer." In those days, children weren't told very
much, if anything. Momma told us she would be back
home soon with "her girls." Momma said there was no
reason to worry. She instructed us to be good girls and
mind and cooperate with everyone who was trying to help
us. This was the first time Momma had ever left us. The
house seemed so empty without her. I missed her terribly.
I didn't know what to do with myself without her. To come
home from school and not find her there was almost

unbearable. I was so lonely. Momma had taught us that we could pray to God about anything. "He is a prayer-answering God," she'd said. So I prayed.

> *God, I want Momma to come back home. God,*
> *please make Momma well and bring her back home to us.*
> *We need her. All I want in the whole wide world is for you*
> *to bring her home. I promise I will be good and mind her.*
> *I will take care of her, God. I will never ask for anything else*
> *if you just bring Momma back home to us.*

I wasn't worried much; I trusted God would bring her back home to us. A few days after her surgery, Momma's friend drove us the 90 miles to Knoxville Hospital to visit her. We were so happy to see her. I was relieved that she was all right. She told us they had operated on her and taken out part of her lung. Momma looked like Momma and was her cheerful self. The only thing I noticed was that her face and arms had gotten darker. Still I saw no reason to be worried. She told us how much she loved "her girls" and that she would be home soon. I couldn't wait for everything to get back to normal. When we got back home that night, I prayed to God.

> *God, thank you for bringing Momma through her surgery.*
> *You do answer our prayers just like Momma said.*
> *God thank you so much for healing Momma.*
> *Please bring her back home to us soon.*
> *Thank you, God!*

A few days later Momma did come home, and for a little while, things were normal again. I was just so happy that we were all back together. I never wanted Momma to leave again. Her love and presence made everything all right.

November 1971

During the next few weeks everything seemed like it was better. Mommas' friends and members from the church and community came by the house and checked on her, bringing cards, flowers and food for the family. I remember one day after school, I went upstairs to check on her and she seemed a little sad. "Are you all right Momma?" I asked. She responded, "Momma is tired and I am tired of putting on a happy face." I had never heard Momma talk like that before. I didn't think much of her comment – I was only 14 years old. I gave her a hug and told her to get some rest and I took her a Coca-Cola.

A few days later Momma took a turn for the worst. She started getting terrible headaches and had to be taken to Pineville Hospital. Again, we weren't told very much, except that Momma was sick and that she had to go back to the hospital for a while. During this time, it became second nature for me to run to God in prayer. It's me again God, I would say.

> Please make Momma well and bring her back home
> to us again. You did it once; please God, do it again.
> Things are not the same when Momma's not here.
> Please, God! We need Momma at home. I don't know
> what is wrong with her. I just know we need her
> home with us. God, please heal Momma.

The next day I was sitting in my classroom when my cousin came and got me from class. He said Dad was in the office waiting for Diane and me. I remember thinking Daddy never came to school, except for ballgames I cheered at. We went home and Daddy told us, "Your Momma is not doing good." It was just like Daddy to not say any more than that. We didn't know what that meant. Did it mean, "*She is not doing good, now, but she will get better soon?*" Or did it mean, "*She is not doing good and she never will be better?*" I was too afraid to ask. I was afraid of the answer. I just wanted to see Momma for myself.

We were taken to the hospital to see Momma. We were met with the familiar antiseptic smell of alcohol mixed with the scent of freshly waxed floors. We had visited Daddy at work many times. We walked into Momma's room and she was lying in her hospital bed. The room was dimly lit. Diane and I immediately went over to give Momma a hug. Something was different about her. It seemed like she was in pain and maybe a little confused. I had never seen Momma like this before. I was immediately distracted by a strange odor in the room. An odor I had never smelled before. It was sweet, strong, and awful at the same time. I remember thinking:

> *Something is really wrong with Momma.*
> *God, please help her now!*

For the first time since Momma's illness I was scared for her - for us.

> *God, can you please help Momma?*
> *I am really afraid.*

In between moments of clarity and confusion, Momma seemed determined to say what was on her mind. "Momma loves you girls two tons," she said, "I want you to be good girls and mind everyone who is trying to help you." She hugged us tightly and told us she loved us over and over again. We didn't get to visit with her long. Before we left we told her we loved her and we wanted her to come home soon. Before leaving the room, she drew me close and whispered to me, "Take care of your sister." What a strange request, I thought. *Of course, I would take care of sis until she got home. Why was she telling me this?*

After leaving the hospital that evening, I was really worried. Nobody was telling us what was really going on and I was afraid to ask. After getting ready for bed that night, I couldn't get Momma off my mind. I had this feeling that something bad was going to happen. I got on my knees as we had done with Momma many times, and I prayed.

> *God, something bad is wrong with Momma. Momma said if we pray to you that you will answer our prayers. I know Momma is right because I prayed for you to bring her home from Knoxville and you did. God, please, please, please make Momma well and bring her home to us. We need her God. We can't live without her.*

I prayed the same prayer over and over again for what seemed like eternity, until I finally dozed off to sleep, sure that everything would be all right in the morning – sure that Momma would be all right because God had heard my prayer.

CHAPTER 6
THE DOORBELL

My God, my God, why have you forsaken me?
Why are you so far from saving me, so far from
my cries of anguish?
~ Psalm 22:1

He who loses his mother, loses a pure soul who blesses
and guards him constantly.
~ Kahlil Gibran

On December 1, 1971, our family found itself thrust into an unfamiliar place – a place of disorientation and confusion. It was an ordinary, cold December morning. I was startled awake by the doorbell around 7:30 a.m., the same doorbell that had rung a hundred times before. I wondered, *who could be at the door so early in the morning?* I could hear the faint voices of Daddy and a local minister. I believe it was Reverend Jones. Then, I remembered. Memories from the previous day came rushing back. I remembered visiting Momma in the hospital and her telling us to be good girls and mind everyone who is trying to help us. I remembered the fear and helplessness I felt at the hospital. I thought back to my prayer the night before – asking God to heal her.

The voices of Daddy and the minister jarred my attention back to the door. The words I heard next would be carved in my mind and heart forever: "I am so sorry to hear about Dorothy's death." The words pierced my soul. My heart sank. I thought, *this must be a mistake. He couldn't be talking about Dorothy, our Momma. Momma would never leave 'her girls.' I must be dreaming. This can't be real. Momma is not dead.* I tried to wake myself up from this nightmare but it wasn't a dream. Daddy was really at the door talking to the minister.

Diane and I raced down the twelve stairs we had played on so many times before. Daddy met us at the bottom of the stairs, still in his crisp white hospital uniform. He was such a tower of strength, standing six feet three inches tall. I will never forget the grief-stricken look on his face. It was deeply troubling to see such a powerful man look so defeated. I had never seen Daddy look so sad.

Daddy took us by the hand and led us into the living room. The living room Momma had decorated so beautifully – teal drapes to match the paisley sofa and pillows. Photographs of Diane and me hung on the wall in gold frames. The bookshelves were filled with books Momma loved to read. The piano she had taught us to play was sitting against the wall with the music book still opened. The piano we had played with Daddy on, even though he could only play one tune. Daddy sat us down. In his usual quiet way, and through tearstained eyes he said, "Girls, your Momma passed away this morning."

She passed away? What do you mean she passed away? Passed away to where? Where is Momma? When is she coming home? I want Momma!

I could hear Daddy talking, but felt like I was floating a million miles away. All I heard was, "Your Momma passed away, your Momma passed away." My mind was trapped somewhere between space and time; I tried to speak, but the words wouldn't come. I wanted to scream, but I had no voice.

God, where were you last night?
Did you not hear my prayer?
I prayed to you and you let Momma die.
What kind of God are you? Where is Momma?
Will you please bring her back to us?
This is just a dream.
It's not too late to bring her home.
Do something now! Please, God!

In that moment, I realized Momma was gone and she wasn't coming back.

I didn't get to tell Momma goodbye.

My mind wandered back to the last time I had seen her. I hadn't seen a woman who was dying. I'd seen my Momma. I didn't want to hear any more from Daddy. I just wanted my Momma. She was the only one who could fix this. I called on God like never before but He had not answered. After the death of his wife to cancer, C. S. Lewis experienced a brief loss of faith. "Where is God?" he wrote in, *A Grief Observed*,[9] "Go to him when your need is desperate, when all other help is vain, and what do you find? A door slammed in your face." I felt that way when Momma died. At fourteen, my childlike trust in God and in life was shattered. The night before Momma passed away, I had prayed in earnest to God as I had done with Momma many times, *God, please make Momma well. Please bring her home to us.* I'd pleaded with God. *God Please! Please don't take our Momma away.*

Momma's passing left me with so many unanswered questions. Questions about her God. I was so confused. I wanted to know:

What kind of God would take away the mother
of two young girls?

Didn't God know how much we needed and depended on her?
We were devastated. Didn't God know that we couldn't
live without our mother? Was this God's plan for our lives?

Since Momma was gone, and Daddy didn't talk about his
faith, the only one left to answer my questions was God
himself.

Part II
Life After Loss

I will lead the blind by ways they have not known,
along unfamiliar paths I will guide them; I will turn
the darkness into light before them and make the rough
places smooth. These are the things I will do;
I will not forsake them.
~ Isaiah 42:16

It is so hard to let go when we lose a loved one.
There is, at first, a great tearing away, a breaking away
of every certainty. Through fluorescent hospital
corridors, sunlit cemeteries and endless condolences,
none of the explanations or prayers seem to suffice. It all
seems unjust, as over the months and years they are not
standing where they should be.
~ Stephen Levine, Unattended Sorrow

CHAPTER 7
MOTHER'S FUNERAL

But now, Lord, what do I look for?
My hope is in you.
~ Psalm 39:7

"There is something about losing your mother that is permanent
and inexpressible – a wound that will never quite heal."
~ Susan Wiggs

December 2, 1971

The morning after Momma passed away, I woke up from
my sleep with my heart racing. I remembered all over
again. At the age of forty-five, Momma was gone. Death
was nothing like I imagined; it was far worse. It was so
final and startling. The one person I wanted, the only one
who could comfort us through this, was gone. And God
was nowhere to be found. I wrote in the pink diary
Momma had given me:

Momma is dead. Momma is gone and she is not coming back.
Today I went shopping for a dress to wear to Momma's funeral.
What do you wear to your mother's funeral? I carefully chose a
navy blue skirt and a top with white trim. Momma would have
liked it. It really wasn't hard finding an appropriate dress
because Momma always picked out pretty dresses
and patent leather shoes for us.

The next few days were a blur. Even now, the more I try to remember, the more memories evade me. I remember waiting for Momma to walk through the door and tell us it was all a mistake - that she would never leave her girls. We gathered at Durham Funeral Home for her wake. In spite of being a cheerleader for Pineville High School, I was shocked and comforted when the entire cheerleading, basketball and football teams, as well as coaches and teachers showed up to pay their respect to a woman many of them didn't even know. My then boyfriend, Fred, Jr., and friends Teresa, Retha, Linda, Curt, Jr., D.C., Drake and many others were close by to support us. Too many friends to count. We felt the arms of the city of Pineville wrap around us. At the wake, Diane and I spent our time talking to our friends and classmates, staying as far as we could from Momma lying in that casket. I thought I saw her breathing a couple of times.

The adults hugged us and told us how sorry they were and that Momma was in a better place.

A better place? I couldn't understand where that better place was. What place could be better than with her daughters and family who desperately needed her?

Some said that God would help us get through this.

We would never get through this I determined; besides, it was God who was responsible. It was God who could have prevented this from happening. But He hadn't.

Others said Momma wouldn't have to suffer any longer. I didn't want Momma to suffer, so this kind of made sense to me. I sensed that everyone was trying to be helpful, but it was not reassuring to know that Momma was in heaven with God, when we needed her here. *Why did God need her so badly?*

December 3, 1971

Momma's funeral was held at Bethel. Our little church was filled to capacity. Everyone in the town, including the mayor, physicians, nurses, friends, neighbors, church members, and family from near and far, were there. I felt the love of the people holding me up. Diane and I sat with Daddy on the first pew. We had never been to a funeral before and had no clue what to expect. It seemed like an ordinary church service, except Momma wasn't at her usual place at the piano. Instead, she was lying in front of us in an open casket. She was dressed in an olive green suit. Green was Momma's favorite color. I wondered if they'd remembered to put patent leather shoes on her feet.

I hate the green suit they have on her. It's the wrong color green. This doesn't seem real. It can't be real. I can't believe Momma is lying there so still. I want her to get up. God, it's not too late for you to bring her back. Momma, please get up. God, please do something! I can't do this. God, this is too hard. Please, please stop this! I want my Momma. We cannot live without Momma. You have to do something God.

Details of Momma's service still escape me. I don't remember the songs, scriptures, or much of what happened. It was as if God placed a protective seal over our tender hearts and minds. After a while, they closed the casket and Pastor Brown began preaching Momma's eulogy. I couldn't breathe when they closed Momma up in that box. It felt like they were closing the lid on my life. What I remember most is the black shiny toupee, sitting almost sideways on the Reverend's head as he preached. I don't remember crying. I was numb and in disbelief of what was happening. My most vivid memory of that day is one I would like to forget, that of Momma lying lifeless in that casket. No child should have to see their mother dead. I distracted myself by looking around at all the beautiful flowers that surrounded Momma's casket and filled the church.

The flowers are so pretty. There are so many. Momma would love them. I don't think I ever bought Momma any flowers, except the dandelions I picked outside in our yard. If I could make one wish today, it would be for Momma to be back at the piano. I would give anything to have her back with us.

The service finally came to an end and so did the life we once knew. The undertakers wheeled Momma's casket to the front door of the church. They reopened her casket and everyone filed past her to express their final goodbyes. It felt as if Momma had been ripped from our arms with no warning or explanation. One day she was home with us, then she was in the hospital, and now she was dead, all within two month's time. I felt weak in my legs and like life had left me too. I didn't want to leave the church. I didn't want to leave Momma alone in her casket. I wanted to go with Momma if she couldn't come back to us.

*How can life go on without Momma?
What's going to happen to Diane and me now?*

Daddy, Diane and I were the last to depart the church. Daddy took us by the hand and led us to Momma. It seemed like a million miles from the front pew to her casket. When we got there, Daddy said, "Kiss your Momma goodbye." I didn't want to kiss her goodbye. I wanted her to get up and come home where she belonged.

*I will never kiss her goodbye.
I will never tell her goodbye.*

But, being the obedient daughters Momma raised us to be, we both kissed Momma. In my heart, though I vowed it was not goodbye. As I leaned over to kiss her, I was startled by the hardness of her face. Her softness was gone.

I missed her touch already.

God, I want Momma's softness back
I want Momma to get up and come home.
God, this is too hard. Why are you doing to this to us?
What kind of God are you?

I don't remember much of what happened after we left the church. I don't remember going to the cemetery for her burial or them putting Momma in the ground. I don't think I could have taken that. I think I would have crawled into the grave with her. Later that day the family gathered at our house on Maple Street. I couldn't stand to be there without Momma. It no longer felt like home. People were laughing, talking and going on as if this was normal.

How can they go on with life?
How can they go on as if this is normal?
Momma is not here and she is not coming back!
Don't they understand? Momma is gone.

There was nothing normal about a mother dying and leaving two daughters behind - motherless. I asked Dee Dee if it was all right if I walked downtown to Newberry's – the local five and ten store. That was the beginning of my shopping addiction and me trying to fill the unbearable emptiness Momma left. It was the beginning of life without Momma.

CHAPTER 8
THE DARKEST NIGHT

Every day I call to you, my God, but you do not answer.
Every night you hear my voice, but I find no relief.
~ Psalm 22:2 (NLT)

Hope is the exception. It comes when circumstances are dire,
when there is considerable uncertainty about how things will
turn out. Hope rises precisely within those moments when fear,
hopelessness or despair seem just as likely.
~ Barbara Fredrickson

December 3, 1971

Night came and I waited for what seemed like an
eternity for Daddy to come home. I just wanted him to tell
me that everything was going to be all right. Diane was
downstairs asleep with Dee Dee. I waited for the light that
usually shone beneath the door in Momma and Daddy's
bedroom. Knowing that only a door separated us from
Momma and Daddy always gave me a sense of being safe
in the world. But now, there was only silence and darkness
where light used to shine through. Even the silence was
loud. I was alone. I wrote in my pink diary. I couldn't find
words to express what I was feeling, so I wrote:

We buried Momma today.
I can't believe she is gone.
I feel so lonely without her.
I feel like part of me is gone, too.
I don't think I can go on without her.
How can we live life without Momma?

I remember thinking how unfair is was that two girls had to bury their mother. There was something terribly wrong with this picture. I tried to go to sleep, but I couldn't. I was suddenly terrified of the dark. Every time I closed my eyes, I saw a vision of Momma in the grave. The house that had once felt like a safe haven was now a scary place. I heard every sound, sounds I had never noticed before. The creaking stairs made me think somebody was coming. I got up to turn the light back on. I was afraid - afraid to go to sleep and afraid to wake back up to reality. I felt so unprotected.

Alone in my bedroom, the tears I had been holding in for days poured down my cheeks. I didn't know why, but I cried out to God.

God, why did you let this happen?
Where were you when Momma died?
Why did you take her away from us?
What is going to happen to us now?
How are we supposed to live our lives without Momma?
This is not supposed to happen. I want Momma.
I can't live life without her. I just want to be with Momma.

In my desperation, I cried out, *God, where are you*? Then it happened. I felt this incredible presence in my bedroom. I felt comforted. It felt like I was being gathered up. Then I heard a whisper, *"Do not be afraid. I am here. I will never leave you. Can you trust me?"* I should have been afraid, but I wasn't. It wasn't a loud booming voice. It was a still, quiet voice. It was undeniable.

Am I going crazy? Is this real?
Is that you God? Where were you when I prayed to you?
Where were you when Momma died?
Why did you let Momma die?

I waited, but there was no answer. Instead, there was just this surprising feeling that everything was going to be all right. I didn't want everything to be all right, I wanted Momma back home with us. I didn't want to feel better about Momma being gone.

I didn't understand exactly what had happened in my bedroom that night. I just knew I wasn't alone. I finally drifted off to sleep.

CHAPTER 9
THE BRAVE GIRL

I call out to the LORD, and he answers me from his holy mountain. I lie down and sleep; I wake again, because the LORD sustains me.
~ Psalm 3:4-5

Your greatest growth in faith will be in moments where all hope seems gone. That's where faith is born and faith births hope. Rest assured, God knows full well what the valley experience will entail, and how long the journey will take to complete His work.
~ Cherie Hill

December 4, 1971

As I woke up the next morning, reality sank in. Momma was really gone. During the course of writing this book, I had a conversation with my dear childhood friend, Mary Ellen. She said, "When your mother passed away, I thought you were the bravest little girl ever." Surprised by her statement, I asked her why she thought I was brave. She said that with courage, I stepped right into my mother's place and began to take care of my family. It was the brave girl that got up the day after her Momma was buried. I didn't feel brave. I just did what I thought Momma would have wanted me to do. Being the oldest daughter, I was willing to forfeit what was left of my childhood for the greater good of the family. Somebody had to go to the grocery store, wash clothes and cook dinner.

Part of me refused to believe Momma was really gone. I would keep going back to her bedroom to see if she was really gone. I knew I couldn't go where she was, so I had to figure out how to go on without her. It was a decision no child should have to make. In truth, I was paralyzed by grief and everyone else in the family was grieving in their own way. I felt the loneliness that Edelman describes, "When a mother dies, the daughter loses her security. When a mother dies, a daughter is starkly alone." My sorrow was too much, so I tucked it neatly away until I could face life without Momma.

Momma's absence left a tear in our hearts and in the fabric of our family. It felt like the heart of our family had stopped beating. In *A Grief Observed*, C. S. Lewis describes his wife's death like this, "Her absence is like the sky, spread over everything." It felt like that when Momma passed away. We had to find a way to go on with life, even though it seemed impossible. Diane and I were lost without her. I still sometimes feel like that vulnerable, motherless little girl in many ways. Diane remembers everyone asking, "Are you all right?" and her response was, "I am fine." Neither one of us had words to express the profound sorrow we were experiencing. We were not fine, but we didn't know how to say it.

The next few weeks and months were hard as we tried to adjust to life without Momma. It was as if she'd just disappeared from the family. Nobody talked about her. The silence was unbearable. We internalized our sorrow because there was nowhere to express it. There was no grief counseling offered to us, which was not uncommon during that time. Everyone went about grieving in their own way. Dee Dee sat in her rocking chair weeping and saying over and over, "Lord have mercy." It was heartbreaking to see this strong woman that had comforted us so many times, so despondent. Daddy went back to work and to his private grieving. The sorrow in his eyes was unbearable. He became even quieter and withdrawn during this time. Diane and I went back to school, to cheerleading, and to our daily routines, secretly guarding the pain in our hearts and minds.

During this time Granny seemed to be the strongest and I leaned on her tremendously and Diane leaned on Dee Dee. I began to spend more and more time at Granny's house next door. My friends, especially Teresa, Retha, and Mary Ellen were a great source of comfort for me. I tried to be strong for everyone, but when I was alone at night, I would weep for Momma and call out to God.

God, I don't know how to go on with life without Momma. You are going to have to help me. Help me to be strong and help me to take care of everyone. Please help me be strong for Diane. God, I am so lonely without Momma. I miss her so much Lord. My heart is breaking. Can you please, please help me? Help my family God, please.

It was such a confusing time. I didn't know what to believe about God. I had sincerely prayed to God to make Momma well. For whatever reason, He did not heal her although it was in his power to do so. I didn't want Momma to suffer, so some part of me could accept her passing. I wasn't in any real danger of not believing in God because I believed Momma. On days that I wanted to give up, I would read my little pink New Testament that Momma had given me. One day I opened my Bible to Jeremiah 29:11-14a: "For I know the plans I have for you," declares the LORD, "plans to prosper you and not to harm you, plans to give you hope and a future. Then you will call on me and come and pray to me, and I will listen to you. You will seek me and find me when you seek me with all your heart. I will be found by you," declares the LORD. It felt like God was speaking directly to me. Even though I was only 14 years old, I clung to those verses - especially the part that said, "I will give you hope and a future."

Life was too hard without Momma. I needed something to hold on to. Harold Smith, in his book, *Grieving the Death of a Mother*,[10] intimated that a mother's last breath inevitably changes us. It is true. I wasn't the same after Momma passed away. This woman who had given us life, nurtured and loved us was gone. I couldn't wrap my mind around her absence. But something (Someone) would not let me give up even though I wanted to. Something was pulling me forward, pulling me to life.

It was difficult to go back to Bethel, but I decided I couldn't stop going just because Momma was gone. I didn't want to disappoint her. Not seeing Momma at the piano was the hardest. It is the place where I'd found the Lord, the place where Momma had taken us. Bethel became a refuge for me during this time. It was a hiding place for my sorrow. It was there that I would slowly begin to grieve as I listened to God's words. It was as if He was speaking directly to me. I heard prayers uttered that gave words to my sorrow – words that I couldn't express. I heard sermons preached that gave me hope to keep going. Not only that, being surrounded by people who loved us was comforting. But it was still very difficult to go on with life.

During the next few months and years, our family adjusted to life without Momma, but we were never the same individually or as a family. I would walk through the house searching for anything left from Momma. They gave away all her things right after she passed away. It never occurred to them that it would have been easier if we had something of hers to hold onto. The house felt so very empty without her. It felt like our house died too.

Daddy eventually found someone else to love. Three years after Momma passed away, he asked us for our blessing to remarry. I felt conflicted. Of course, I wanted him to be happy; I just didn't want him to replace Momma. At the same time, I loved him and didn't want him to be alone, so I gave my blessing. Dad was only 41, with a lot of life to live. I also thought it would be good for Diane to have someone to love and support her. Yet I vowed that no one would ever take Momma's place and I would never call anyone else Momma again. I felt it would be disloyal to Momma.

Dad's wife, Geneva and I developed a relationship and she did all she could to support Diane and me. She was good to us. We actually became friends rather than "stepdaughter and stepmother." They started their own family and together they had a son, Steven and a daughter, Rebecca. A new generation of Turners would continue to grow from their union. Later their grandchildren, Alex, Jacob, and Genesia and their great-grandchildren Madison and Maleigha would be born. I was happy to have another little sister and a brother. I was glad Daddy had a family, although I secretly wished for Momma to still be here. I would have given anything to have her back with us.

Dee Dee moved across town, which was devastating because she was our continuity between the past and the present and life before and after Momma. When she left, the house felt even emptier. She had been with us even before we were born. We missed her terribly when she moved, especially Diane. It was another loss that we would grieve. I spent most of my days at our house and nights with Granny and Diane spent a lot of her time with Dee Dee. God had given both of us a hiding place. Sleeping in the bedroom next to Granny was comforting and provided a sense of security for me. I still believed in God, I had to, but I had no idea what kind of plan he had for my life.

CHAPTER 10
A FAMILY OF MY OWN

As a mother comforts her child,
so will I comfort you.
~ Isaiah 66:13a

One joy shatters a hundred griefs.
~ Chinese Proverb

Hope Edelman describes motherless daughters as "perennial mourners: always longing, hoping, and searching for her love, her touch, and her voice." The void in my heart marked by Momma's absence was unbearable. In my search for Momma's love, I found Michael. A year or so after Momma passed away, I met Michael and my dear friend Saundra at a school dance at Union College, which was 18 miles from Pineville. Michael was from Versailles, Kentucky and had been attending Union College since 1972. I had no idea when I first met him that he would be the man that God had chosen to be the father of my children and husband. His smile and his tender heart won me over and I fell in love hard and fast. My family loved him as well.

On March 8, 1974 I gave birth to my beautiful daughter, Penny Lane. I remember feeling the reality of Momma's absence sorely on that day. I cried for Momma as I gave birth to her first granddaughter. It was bittersweet. When I first saw Penny, my heart was filled with joy again. She was the most precious bundle of love. She looked just like Granny. We should have named her Hope because that was what she was for me. She brought happiness and joy back to me and to our family. I had a lot of support from Dad and Geneva, Diane, everyone in my family as well as my friends. But it was my grandmother and Michael that helped me the most.

I knew Momma would have loved Michael, as everyone in the family did. Michael, whose name means, "one like God," was truly God-sent in my life. He was a kind and gentle man. Now we did party and have a good time but it was evident that Michael loved the Lord. He would wake everyone up in his dorm and tell them, "Come on, it's time to go to church." After Dad met him, he asked, "Are you going to marry him?," which was his way of giving his blessing. And I did marry him. I would find out years later that Granny, who loved Michael tremendously, had instructed him to take care of "her girls."

Being responsible for another human being fueled me with purpose and meaning. In some strange way being a mother strengthened the bond with my own mother, although she was gone. My friend Retha's mother, Daisy, was Penny's babysitter for a while and she loved Penny like she was her own. After I enrolled in Union College in Barbourville, which was 18 miles from home, Granny kept Penny. I commuted back and forth with my friend Pam Walters until we eventually moved there.

That same year I witnessed Dad getting baptized in Middlesboro. Momma would have been so happy. Her prayers had been answered. She would have enjoyed hearing Dad sing in the choir and seeing him as a trustee of the church. I wondered if their lives would have been better if they had been able to serve the Lord together.

Michael, Penny and I moved to Lexington in 1979. It was especially difficult leaving behind the people I loved and who loved me, but I felt myself being pulled toward the future. It broke my heart to leave my little sis, Diane, but I prayed that God would watch over her and take care of her. As I write this book, Michael and I have been together over 42 years. We have had our share of ups and downs, but through it all, we never gave up on each other or the love that is between us.

I gained a new family in Lexington. Michael's Mom, Stella and Dad, Charles and his Aunt Peaches, became dear to me. Stella and Peaches were like no women I had been around before. They both were tough and tender. Strong, outspoken and generous. Stella would become more than a mother-in-law, but a mother-in-love. She taught me to be courageous and confident. To speak my mind and to not worry about anything. She loved the Lord and didn't mind telling anyone. She was a hard-working woman that gave everything she had to her children. Over the years, we would become close. I would call her "Mom" and she called me, "My Lynn."

Charles, like Michael, was soft-spoken, a gentleman. He worked as a hospital orderly, just like my Dad. I remember thinking he was the jolliest man I had ever met. He loved spending time with his grandchildren and tinkering around in his workshop. The two of them, along with Michael's sister Ann and his brother Doug, would form a strong support network for our family. Doug and his wife Monica had two children Nicole and Doug II. Over the next couple of years, Diane, Dee Dee, and my best friend, Teresa, moved to Lexington. It felt good to have family in Lexington with me.

Michael and I joined Pleasant Green Baptist Church and they became family to us. Pastor Peoples and the church supported our family through the many joys, deaths, births, graduations and illnesses we experienced in life. Women like Mrs. Sidney Bell Johnson, Mrs. Mary Wilson, Mrs. Mayme Wheeler, Mrs. Delma Peoples and many more became mother-figures in my life as they shared their woman wisdom with me. God was definitely ordering my steps, even though it would take years for me to understand all the ways.

During this time, I still missed Momma terribly and wrestled with why God had not healed her. I longed for her presence, her wisdom, and her touch. Some days I would not want to get out of bed, I missed her so much. Being a motherless daughter was hard. Yet, I had so much to be grateful for. I still had questions about what kind of God would allow such suffering, but at the same time, I could see how God was blessing us. Being a mother somehow soothed the heartbreak of not having my mother with me. Being a wife gave me arms to hold me. God had given me a family of my own. God had given me people for my life.

CHAPTER 11
HEART BROKEN

I wait for the LORD, my whole being waits,
and in his word I put my hope. I wait for the Lord more
than watchmen wait for the morning, more than
watchmen wait for the morning.
~ Psalm 130:5-6

Your most profound and intimate experiences
of worship will likely be in your darkest days – when your heart
is broken, when you feel abandoned, when you're out of options,
when the pain is great – and you turn to God alone.
~ Rick Warren

April 1982

I ran down the corridor of the hospital to the emergency room where they would be bringing Granny. I'd received a telephone call from Daddy earlier that day letting me know they were rushing Granny by ambulance from Pineville to St. Joseph Hospital in Lexington. Daddy said he would come later on. My mind raced back to all those times Granny had been rushed to the hospital in Pineville. Each time, I'd thought she wouldn't make it, but each time God had brought her through. I knew it was His grace that had kept her. I would always pray, *God please bring her back to us.* This time was no different. While waiting for the ambulance to arrive, I went to the hospital chapel to pray:

God, it's me again. You brought Granny through many heart
attacks. Please Lord, I trust and believe you can
make her well. Lord, we can't lose another person so precious to
us. It would be too much. It was bad enough that we lost
Momma; God please don't take Granny too.
We need her God. Please, God, please heal Granny! She is
everything to me, Diane, Penny and our whole family.
God, please heal her heart.

Granny finally arrived and was rushed to the Intensive
Care Unit. The heart specialist told us she was in
congestive heart failure and that she probably would not
make it through the night. We were so afraid we were
going to lose her this time. Granny's sister, Aunt Pauline
from Maryland, arrived the next day and it was good to
have family there with us. Being in the hospital with
Granny brought back memories of Momma. I wanted
Momma – to run to her arms and for her to tell me
everything was going to be all right. I was definitely feeling
the magnitude of the moment.

We were told to go home and rest and that they would
run additional tests in the morning. I reluctantly agreed,
not knowing what would happen to Granny. I found
myself on my knees again, praying to God. I didn't know
if I could trust Him with Granny; He had already allowed
Momma to die. I couldn't believe this was happening
again. It brought up all the sorrow from losing Momma.
It revived the pain that I had stuffed deep inside.

God, this can't be happening again!
Please do something, God. I am so afraid.
I am afraid that I can't trust you with Granny.
I still believe in you.
I know you have the power to make her well;
I just don't know if you will.
Lord, please, you can't take Granny from us!
Please let her be there in the morning.

God was merciful and heard my prayer; Granny made it through the night. I was so grateful to God.

God thank you for bringing Granny through the night. You are a good God and I am so grateful that you kept her here with us. You know how much we need her.

Throughout the day, they ran diagnostic tests on Granny to determine the course of treatment. Aunt Pauline decided to leave the hospital to run some errands and asked me to go with her. I refused to leave. I would not abandon the woman who had been there for me and my daughter. After Momma passed away, I vowed that I would never allow a loved one to pass away without me being there for them, as if I was a death angel and God needed me to assist Him with His work. I was determined I would not miss saying goodbye ever again.

Aunt Pauline left and it was just the two of us – Granny and me. It was our time. I said, "Granny I love you so much and appreciate everything you did to help me and Penny. You have been my safe place in the world since I was a little girl. Penny loves you so much and you have been such a great influence in both of our lives." In turn, Granny shared how much she loved me, Diane, Penny and Dr. Hayes who was like family to her.

Little did I know this would be our last conversation, the last time I would be able to tell her how much she meant to me. We talked about her staying on in Lexington with us while she recuperated. She then said, "Take care of my baby." Then Granny sat straight up in the bed, fell back and died. I witnessed Granny take her last breath. I felt helpless as the nurses came in to work with her. I rushed to the phone to call Michael, who came right away. He was such a source of strength to me as the nurses told me what I already knew that Granny had indeed passed away.

Ten years after losing our mother, we lost the woman who had been like a mother to us. She was our GRAND-mother. My heart was broken all over again. I called Daddy to tell him that his mother had passed away. He had now lost the two most important women in his life. I could not believe that God had again allowed someone so dear to us to pass away. At the ages of 22 and 24, Diane and I had lost the two most important people in our lives. It was too much. I understood less and less about God.

God, why? We already lost Momma.
I don't understand why you let Granny die, too.
I know it was in your power to make her well.
I believe that. God, I don't understand you at all or
how you decide when to heal someone and when to allow
them to pass on - how you decide who gets to live.
I can't do this. You took Momma away and now
Granny too. It is too hard to say goodbye to Granny.
Lord, please help me through this.
Help our family Lord, please.

We arranged for Granny's remains to be taken back to Pineville for her funeral and burial. I was in shock and disbelief as we prepared for her service. I remember when the undertakers came to our house on Maple Street to pick the family up to drive us to Bethel. I couldn't get up or move. I didn't want to see another person I loved in a casket. I wanted Momma. Daddy came over to me and took my hand and said, "Let's go." It was his strength that got me through that day.

Losing Granny sent me running to God for answers. I needed to understand who He really was. I needed God to help me make sense of the suffering and sorrow that was mine to bear. It was during this time that I really began seriously seeking the Lord and He became nearer and dearer to me.

CHAPTER 12
HERITAGE

Children are a heritage from the LORD,
offspring a reward from him.
~ Psalm 127:3

In the night of death, hope sees a star,
and listening love can hear the rustle of a wing.
~ Robert Ingersoll

The cycle of death and birth, endings and beginnings and winters and springs, became evident in the life of our family. Four months after Granny passed, Diane gave birth to my niece, Erica. She had the most beautiful brown eyes and reminded me of Dee Dee. She had her spunk and spirit. I found out I was pregnant during this time. It was a difficult pregnancy with pre-eclampsia and subsequent complications. I was hospitalized for a week before my physician decided to perform a cesarean section. During this time, I longed for both Momma and Granny. Lying in the hospital bed on complete bed rest, I found myself praying, again, to the Lord, who was becoming like a mother to me.

Lord, it's me again. God, please protect our baby and let
her be born healthy. God, please restore my health so that
I will be able to take care of her. I trust you with my life and
with our baby's life. Please let me give birth to a healthy baby.

One year and seven days after we buried Granny, I gave birth to our second daughter, April. She brought a new season of joy to me and to our family. "Her name is April," Michael said, "to represent spring and new life." I could see my mother in her and he could see his grandmother. Our family was complete and I was overcome with joy and gratitude.

God, I am so thankful that you brought me through this pregnancy. Thank you for the gift of another daughter. Thank you for your care during my pregnancy and birth. I know it is because of your grace that she is here and that we are both healthy. Thank you Lord for restoring joy to me and my family.

I was beginning to notice a pattern of God's grace and hope being born each time we experienced a devastating loss. It was like God was showing me His hand in the midst of death and loss; His hand of mercy and His tender loving care. He had become like a mother to me. I was beginning to see who God really was and to trust Him more. My childlike faith was growing into a more mature and enduring faith.

This pattern of giving birth after a major loss became a theme in my life. About 9 months after I gave birth to April I graduated from the University of Kentucky with a bachelor's degree in Social Work. Momma and Granny would have been so proud. It was bittersweet because they weren't there to witness the first college graduation in our family. In the midst of celebrating my achievement, all I wanted was Momma. I went to bed that day and cried instead of going to my graduation because Momma was not there. I was experiencing what Levin describes in his book, *Unattended Sorrow*,[11] "The ability to cognitively understand and comprehend the loss of a mother only comes from numerous times of bumping against reality. She is not here, she is not here – as we go through life and miss her and want to see her or to hold her and she is not with us."

I was learning to deal with the duality of life as I bumped up against the reality of Momma not being here. I was learning that life is a full mixture of joy and sorrow. I knew it was by the grace of God that I had been able to complete my degree while working and raising children. I was learning to embrace Momma's God as my God. It was only through walking with her God that I began to know and understand Him for myself.

Several years later Diane gave birth to her son, my nephew Joshua. He looked just like Daddy and today, he has his mannerisms. Our family continued to grow as Michael's sister, Ann miraculously gave birth to our nephew Idongesit, who only weighed 4 pounds when he was born. He wasn't expected to survive. I was beginning to see God's grace shining on our family. Even though we had all made our own mistakes, I could see that God can, and does, work out all things for our good. We may not be able to see the good when we are going through it, but He sees it all. I am still surprised when He shows his Hand in the midst of death – surprised by the moments of grace and how a tiny seed of hope can blossom into full joy. The same well in which sorrow flows is the same place where joy emerges.

CHAPTER 13
SUNRISE

*Bend down, O LORD, and hear my prayer;
answer me, for I need your help. Be merciful to
me, O Lord, for I am calling on you constantly.*
~ Psalm 86:1, 3 (NLT)

My sun sets to rise again.
~ Elizabeth Barrett Browning

August 1994

Michael and I were busy working and raising our
children – shuttling them to and from school, ball games
and church. Meanwhile, I was back in school working on
my master's degree. It seemed every time I lost someone
close to me, I had to birth something, a baby or a degree.
After having two beautiful daughters, degrees became my
preferred method of giving birth. My family and I were in
a season of orientation. Things were going well when Dee
Dee suddenly had a stroke and was hospitalized. Her
doctors told us she would probably not survive overnight.
She lay in her hospital bed unresponsive for almost a week.

During that time, Diane and I talked with her, read
scriptures and prayed for her. Panic set in as I faced the
probability of saying goodbye to another one I loved
dearly.

Lord, here we are again. I know that you have the power of life and death in your hands. I am praying you will not take Dee Dee away from us. God, we still need her. Can't you please leave her with us for a little while longer? God, you have Momma and Granny; please don't take Dee Dee, too.

God answered our prayers. Dee Dee came out of the coma and Michael and I took her home to care for her as she recuperated. She needed daily assistance and being the strong and independent woman she was, insisted on going to a nursing home. She worried she was a burden on our family, in spite of us telling her it was a privilege, not a burden to care for her. She was convinced she was dying and kept saying, "I don't want to die in your home." She would not rest until we followed her wishes. Therefore, we reluctantly took her to Pine Meadows Nursing Home.

I received a call at work a few weeks later indicating that Dee Dee had taken a turn for the worse. She was more than our aunt; she was our history. Dee Dee had been our stability and sense of familiarity – she'd been with us from birth to now. She was 94 years old, though, and ready to go. She told us this on many occasions: "I don't know why the Lord has kept me here. I don't know why He won't take me home." I believe He had not taken her home because we still needed her a little while longer. We needed time to say goodbye. Letting go of Dee Dee was like letting go of our past. It felt like letting go of pieces of Momma too.

I knew I needed to change my prayer, but I didn't want her to leave us. During her last days, Diane and I spent the hours at her bedside, laughing, talking and reminiscing about all the good times we'd had together. Our pastor, Reverend Peoples, came by and offered a prayer for her. I still remember him reading from Psalm 27:1: "The Lord is my light and my salvation, whom shall I fear. The Lord is the strength of my life." I remember parts of his prayer like it was yesterday. Especially the part in which he prayed, "Thy will be done." I didn't want God's will to be done.

I wanted God to make Dee Dee well. I had sat with impending death enough times to know it wouldn't be long until she closed her eyes to us forever. I prayed, asking God to give me strength to say goodbye to a woman who had meant so much to me and to our family. It was especially hard for my sister because Dee Dee had become like a mother to her.

God, it's me. Here we are again, at a crossroad.
I know it is in your power to heal Dee Dee.
I just don't know if it's your will. You, alone,
get to decide. I know she is ready to go. She has
been ready for so long, so Lord, if it is her time,
if it is your will, please give us strength to tell her
goodbye. God please give us strength to let go.

I was surprised to hear my own prayer. I was praying God's will be done and asking God for strength to accept whatever His plan was for Dee Dee's life. I was surprised by the strength God gave me to say what needed to be said. With tears in my eyes, I said, "Dee Dee you know how much we love you. You have been so good to us. We appreciate everything you have done for us. I want you to know that we are going to be all right because God is going to take care of us. It is okay for you to rest now and go home to be with the Lord. We will see you again, soon."

I knew it was the Lord who had given me and Diane strength to tell Dee Dee how much she had meant to us and to say goodbye. She needed us to tell her goodbye so that she could let go. When it came time to leave Pine Meadows, I held her hands and told her how much I loved her as I kissed her on the cheek. I said, "I'll be back in the morning," when suddenly the unthinkable happened. She pushed my hands away. I was devastated and hurt by this gesture. This woman who had loved us, rocked us and cared for us from birth, had gently pushed me away. The same hands that had taught me how to cook were now pushing me away.

What I now understand is that Dee Dee was encouraging me not to cling to her, but to cling to Jesus. The Lord gave me strength to walk out of her room that night, leaving her in His watchful care and capable hands. I was learning that God did not need my assistance transitioning His children home, not that he ever did. That night I prayed to Him:

God, I know Dee Dee's life is in your hands. Selfishly, I don't want her to leave us. She has meant so much to us. But she is tired and she is ready to go. I am asking that you give me strength and courage to accept your will. God please comfort her and gently accept her in your arms. Please carry her home safely Lord. She is precious to us.

The next morning I woke up early and went for my usual walk in my neighborhood. This was my time to talk to God. I planned to go back to Pine Meadows to visit Dee Dee later that morning. I walked right into the sun rising from the east. For a brief moment, the sun beamed directly on my face. The warmth from the sun was incredible. It was in that moment that I knew – Dee Dee was gone. I felt her leaving. When I arrived at home, I received a call from the nursing home telling us she had passed away a few minutes earlier. All I could say was, "Lord, have mercy"- a phrase we had heard Dee Dee use so many times. She was now at rest, at peace - at home.

God gave us strength to take Dee Dee home to Bethel for her funeral and burial. I was very sad, but at peace, held up and strengthened by the Lord. Daddy was also a reassuring presence for us during this time, helping to make funeral arrangements and to take care of the details. Diane and I shopped for a beautiful teal dress to bury her in. There was something about carefully choosing her dress that helped us to let go.

Surrounded by family and friends, we then said goodbye to Dee Dee, burying her with loving care as she had lovingly cared for us all our lives. The three women that first knew, loved and nurtured us from birth had gone on before us. There was something unbearable about their absence and something beautiful about realizing they were all together now. I opened my Bible that evening to II Corinthians 12:9, which reads, "But He said unto me, 'My grace is sufficient for you, for my power is made perfect in weakness.' Therefore I will boast all the more gladly about my weaknesses, so that Christ's power may rest upon me."

CHAPTER 14
GENERATIONAL BONDS

Thou hast put gladness in my heart.
~ Psalm 4:7a (NLT)

*My grandchildren are a window to my past, a mirror of today,
a door to tomorrow and the keeper of my heart for all eternity.*
~ Unknown

After Dee Dee passed away I remember telling Michael, "I am not having any more babies." The pattern of having a baby every time I lost someone dear would have to stop there. To my surprise and shock, ten months after Dee Dee passed away, I witnessed the birth of my first granddaughter, Candace. We had sent Penny off to the University of Kentucky to get a degree, and instead, she got us our first granddaughter. She did earn her Bachelor's degree in education later and we were so proud of her. As I witnessed Candace being born, I was in awe of God's tender mercy and grace. I had been privileged to witness my grandmothers' last breath and my granddaughters' first. I felt tremendously blessed to witness both sacred moments.

I fell in love as soon as I saw my first granddaughter; she was such a gentle spirit. She looked just like Penny, and at the same time, Granny. It was as though my grandmother's face was transposed on her face and my grandmother was being born again. I couldn't tell where Candace began and my grandmother ended. When I left the hospital that day, I looked and felt like I had given birth. Something spectacular had happened.

A year and a few months later, Penny gave birth to our second granddaughter, Maya. I was in love again. The blood and the thread that ran from generation to generation was undeniable. Maya looked just like Dee Dee and entered the world with all her sass and strength. I sensed she was an old soul. I experienced the joy of witnessing something my mother was never able to: the birth of my grandchildren. I was so grateful to God.

Being a mother and a grandmother have been the greatest joys of my life. I sometimes think I have been living my mother's dreams for her. I love my family for letting me hold on too tight, for loving too hard sometimes. I think in many ways I've become the mother I longed for. I've loved enough for two people – both Momma and me.

My daughters filled my life with hope, purpose and joy. My grandchildren, who call me Nana, have taught me to play again, to imagine new possibilities and most of all to love from that same deep well of grief I'd been carrying around. When Candace and Maya turned fourteen, the age I was when Momma passed away, I saw myself at that age for the first time. Through my granddaughters, I got of glimpse of the 14-year-old me. Through their bright eyes and innocence, I could at last cry for that little girl who had tried to be strong for everyone else. I could finally grieve for that little girl who had to say goodbye to her mother way too soon. Through motherhood and grand-parenting I came to realize:

I am my mothers' daughter
My mother is me
I am my daughters' mother
My daughters are me
I am my granddaughters' grandmother
My granddaughters are me
Heart to heart
Breast to breast
We are one
Forever bonded together
Five generations linked together
through blood and love
Forever linked together by the past,
present and the future
I am my mother's daughter
My mother is me
I am my mother
My mother is me.

CHAPTER 15
HEART FIXER

*My flesh and my heart faileth: but God is the strength
of my heart, and my portion forever.*
~ Psalm 73:26

*God is the way-maker and burden-bearer, a heart-fixer and a
mind regulator. He is my all in all, my everything.*
~ Sister Thea Bowman

In the fall of 1996, I received a call from Pineville Hospital to inform me that they were rushing Dad by ambulance to Central Baptist Hospital in Lexington because he was in heart failure. Central Baptist is only three miles from my house, so I went right away and waited for what seemed like an eternity for the ambulance to arrive with Dad. Diane was a nursing assistant at Central Baptist at the time, so we waited together for them to bring Dad. When he arrived, he was unresponsive. I was sure that Daddy was already gone and that I had missed the opportunity to tell him goodbye.

After diagnostic tests, the heart surgeon found that Dad had 98 percent blockage in the main artery to his heart and blockages in other arteries as well. We were told he would not survive if they didn't do surgery right away. There was not much time to decide; Daddy's life was in peril. I raced to the hospital chapel and prayed. I felt like that little 14-year-old girl who had lost her mother so many years ago.

With guilt, I recalled asking God why He hadn't taken Daddy instead of Momma after she'd died because we'd needed her more. And now, here we were, losing Daddy and I regretted those thoughts with everything in me.

Growing up in Bethel I'd heard the elders say, "God is a heart fixer and a mind regulator." As a child, I'd had no idea what they meant. But after living a while and journeying through life without Momma, Granny, and Dee Dee, I'd understood. God was, indeed, both a mind regulator and a heart fixer. He regulates our minds to accept the unexplainable and fixes our heart to bear the unbearable. There in that hospital chapel, I prayed:

> *God, I know you to be a heart fixer and Daddy's heart needs fixing. God, please, please don't take Daddy. There are so many things I want to say to him. God, please don't take him before I can tell him how much he means to me. God, please bring him through the surgery, if it is your will. God, please let Daddy live. We need more time with Daddy. Please God, please!*

Dad and Geneva had divorced a few years earlier and since I was the eldest, I had to sign the consent form for his heart surgery. Then, they took Dad away. It was the longest five hours of our lives, but Dad made it through the quadruple by-pass surgery. I was so grateful to God for answering our prayers. God let Daddy live. We were told the surgery could possibly extend his life by 10 years or more. And it did.

As we visited Dad in the recovery room, the first words from his mouth were, "Who signed for me to have heart surgery?" I confessed it was me who'd given consent and that he wouldn't be here with us if I had not. He seemed to appreciate being alive, but let me know not to sign for any more surgeries. I had not even considered whether he'd wanted life-saving measures. It's a conversation we'd never had before.

It was a long recovery for Dad. After leaving the hospital, he was in a rehabilitation center for weeks. Michael and I brought him to our home to care for him after he left the rehabilitation center; Diane helped when she could. He was with us for nine months. During this time I was working on my Ph.D. It was a challenging season, going to school and caring for Dad and family, but I was so grateful for the time we had together. I cherished it. We talked and laughed and forgave. As I cared for Dad, I became reacquainted with the man I'd loved as a little girl. A man who had always been there the best he could, giving as much as he could. I realized I had held him to a standard of perfection that nobody, especially myself, could live up to. I saw him now, not as a perfect man, but as a loving father.

God, please forgive me for being so self-righteous and judgmental. Forgive me for blaming and judging Daddy, when I have my own mistakes and sins before me.

After nine months with us, Dad was ready to go back home to Pineville. He missed home and family. I reluctantly took him back to the mountains that he loved. I was so grateful to God for not only restoring him back to health but for renewing our relationship as father and daughter.

CHAPTER 16
HOPEVILLE

*But in my distress I cried out to the LORD; yes, I prayed to my
God for help. He heard me from his sanctuary;
my cry to him reached his ears.*
~ Psalm 18:6 (NLT)

*The natural flights of the human mind are not from pleasure to
pleasure, but from hope to hope.*
~ Samuel Johnson

2002

Things were going well for our family. I finally
completed my Ph.D., and life was beginning to settle down.
That same year April graduated from the University of
Kentucky with a bachelor's degree and we were so proud.
That's when Penny developed a persistent cough. After a
lung biopsy and further testing by a lung specialist, it could
not be determined exactly what was wrong with her. I was
overcome with fear as I remembered Momma's persistent
cough and her dying from lung cancer. In later years we
learned that Momma had small cell lung cancer and that
the cancer had metastasized to her brain. The faith and
trust in God that I'd developed by that point had come
with a price - the price of losing those I loved. As Penny
coughed, I prayed,

Here we go again, God. I cannot lose another person
I love, especially not our daughter. You must know this,
Lord. This is the child that you gave us. Please don't take her
from me. God, please don't let her have cancer. It is in your
power to make her well. I believe you can make her well.
I just don't know if you will. I am so afraid you will choose not
to. I know you can hear me. I know you answer prayer because
you have answered so many other prayers. I have already lost
so many that I loved. God, please don't take her away. Please,
God, don't leave her children motherless. Please help the doctors
find out what is wrong with her and please heal her Lord.

My faith seemed to be failing me. I vacillated between believing God would heal her and fearing He wouldn't. Because God had not healed Momma and Granny, I did not trust Him with my daughter. The tug-of-war I'd had with God over the years was in full effect; me holding on and trying to control the outcome, and God urging me to cling to Him and not my loved ones. I remember talking with my pastor and telling him I could not take it if God took my daughter away from us. He told me I had to trust God's will for her life and that through God's grace and help, we would face whatever was before us. This was not what I wanted to hear. I wanted to hear that God would not take her away from us.

God, it's me again. I come to you in earnest,
asking you to please heal our daughter. God, I can't lose her.
I have lost the three most important people in my life.
I am sorry my faith is wavering. I know it seems like
I don't trust you with the daughter that you gave me.
I know she belongs to you and that your will must be done.
I just don't know what your will is and I am sorry to say,
I don't trust your will. Lord, I believe,
please help my unbelief.

Penny showed tremendous strength and faith in God during this time. It was my first glimpse into the depth of her quiet, yet determined faith. She recently shared with me that she was really worried, but hid it from us. She said, "I was alone at home one day, upset and crying. All of a sudden, this peace came over me. I stopped crying. I knew I was going to be ok. God was telling me that I would be all right." She then went on with her life, raising her girls and trusting in God while I secretly fell apart inside.

We were in and out of the emergency room and doctors' offices as they tried to figure out why she had damage at the base of her lungs. I tried to keep up a good front, but I was being held together by her confidence in God, and my husband's as well. I lived on borrowed faith during this time. I beat myself up for not being stronger and for not trusting God more. But the track record I had with God and my loved ones was not good. Since the physicians in Lexington could not diagnose her, I asked (or rather, demanded) that they refer her to Mayo Clinic. With a love offering and prayers from our church, we rented a van, loaded up the family and drove the 718 miles to Mayo Clinic in Rochester, Minnesota.

We were met by God's grace and the most amazing doctors, nurses, and staff at Mayo Clinic. Instead of being called Mayo Clinic, my husband and I started calling it Hopeville. Everywhere we went in the hospital and the surrounding community, we were met with such kindness. The team of physicians at Mayo were able to diagnose her illness and to put her on a treatment plan that included chemotherapy and a regime of medications to prevent further damage to her lungs. Taking her to Mayo Clinic saved her life; I felt so ashamed that I hadn't trusted God.

God, please forgive me for not trusting you with Penny.
You created her and you love her. She is your daughter.
You have a purpose and a plan for her life that can't be controlled by me. Who am I to try and control the outcome of her life when she belongs to you? God, you gave her to us but she belongs to you. Lord thank you for being so merciful to me and my family.

Our daughter's illness was yet another lesson in letting go and letting God. Another lesson in trusting God. God let me know that Penny's sickness was not unto death. He was working things out for our good even in the midst of uncertainty and doubt. I was reminded of Jesus' response to Mary and Martha when they sent word that Lazarus, whom Jesus loved, was sick and in need of healing. Jesus responded in John 11:4: "This sickness is not unto death, but for the glory of God, that the Son of God might be glorified thereby."

As I sat there at Mayo Clinic, I thought back to that lonely night in my bedroom, the night I realized Momma was not coming back. I cried out to God and He asked, "Can you trust me?" Learning to trust and depend on Him has been a lifelong journey of Him walking with me through many of life's disappointments. He has never let me down. Not only did God restore Penny's health; He allowed me to see His hand of mercy on her life.

Today, Penny is doing well. She went back to Mayo Clinic for a check-up a few years ago and they were pleased to report no further damage to her lungs. When the doctors at Mayo Clinic informed us she would not be able to have any more children following the chemotherapy treatments, I understood why she'd had her daughters when she did. If she hadn't, my granddaughters wouldn't be here today. During this time my faith in God became stronger and I really desired to walk even closer to Him. Not only because He had restored Penny's health, but because He has never left or forsaken me just as He promised.

CHAPTER 17
GETTIN' TO HEAVEN

Lord, hear my voice; let thine ears be attentive to the voice of my supplications. I wait for the Lord, my soul doth wait and in his word do I hope.
~ Psalm 130: 2,5

Death and love are the two wings that bear
the good man to heaven.
~ Michelangelo

My father-in-law, Charles Smith, whom we called "Big Pop" was diagnosed with lung cancer, in July of 2004. It was my privilege to accompany him to some of his visits to the hospital for chemotherapy. During our time together we talked a lot about his illness. On one particular day, he asked me if he was dying. Startled, I answered the best I could by telling him the Lord is the only one who knows when we are going home to be with Him. "The doctors can give their best diagnosis," I said, "but it's really just their best prediction. They don't know when the Lord will call you home. Only the Lord knows."

On one particular day, Big Pop passed out in the wheelchair as I was wheeling him into the Veteran's Hospital. I prayed, Lord, please don't let him pass away right here. I knew my mother-in-love, Stella would say, "I know Lynn killed Charles." God was on our side that day. Staff from the hospital came to help and discovered that his blood sugar had dropped too low.

The hospital visits with Big Pop taught me a lot about God's timing. As his condition worsened in hospice, we had another conversation about the Lord and heaven. Big Pop said, "I want to go to heaven, but I don't want to die to get there." Isn't that how most of us feel? We want our eternal home to be with the Lord, but if we had our choice, the chosen vehicle would not be death. My father-in-law had a Christian's hope of eternal life; he just didn't want to die to get there.

During his last days, Michael and I read scriptures to him, including the following passage from Psalm 27:1-2, 4-5: "The Lord is my light and my salvation - whom shall I fear? The Lord is the stronghold of my life - of whom shall I be afraid? One thing I ask from the Lord, this only do I seek: that I may dwell in the house of the Lord all the days of my life, to gaze on the beauty of the Lord and to seek him in his temple. For in the day of trouble he will keep me safe in his dwelling; he will hide me in the shelter of his sacred tent and set me high upon a rock." I found myself praying to the Lord again.

I come on behalf of my father-in-law. Lord, I come to
you trusting that you know what he stands in need of.
If it is your will, please heal him. If it is your will to take him
home to be with you, please guide him safely into your arms.
God please give us strength to accept your will.

It was as if God was teaching me how to sit with death, to be a midwife for those transitioning from death to life. This is not the assignment I envisioned for my life. My father-in-law quietly passed away early in the morning of September 7, 2004. Prior to passing, the only two things he wanted were peppermint patties, which I gave him plenty of, and to go home. He'd say, "Michael I just want to go home." Going home seems to be the greatest longing of those who are dying. Maybe, just maybe, the home they long for is not a house, nor the sentimental place they resided in on earth, but their eternal home with their Heavenly Father.

Thou hast made us for thyself, and our heart
is restless until it finds its rest in thee.
~ Augustine, Confessions

CHAPTER 18
A BRUISED REED

A bruised reed he will not break, and a
smoldering wick he will not snuff out.
In faithfulness he will bring forth justice.
~ Isaiah 42:3

In my deepest, darkest moments, what really got me through was
a prayer. Sometimes my prayer was simply, 'Help me.'
~ Iyanla Vanzant

In June of 2006, I received a telephone call from my
cousin, Deborah saying, "Your Uncle Barton is on his front
porch with the state police pointing guns at him." I
wondered how this could be. How could this quiet and
gentle man we'd loved since we were little girls end up on
his porch with guns pointed at him? My cousin wanted to
know if I could try to call and talk to him. Before I had a
chance, however, she called back to tell me, "They shot
him." I didn't even have time to pray, except for, *Lord have*
mercy on Uncle Bart. I thought back to all those times he'd
come by Granny's house on Maple Street bringing bags of
groceries and treats for Penny. How could this tender-
hearted man, who'd never bothered anyone, end up
leaving the earth this way? Now, he wasn't perfect. He did
own guns and would occasionally shoot a warning shot in
the air if he thought someone was trespassing on his
property at night. That said, his house had been broken

into many times and he was rightly suspicious of his neighbors.

Later that evening we learned more of the story. Uncle Bart had gone out on his porch with his shotgun, as per usual, to check on things in his yard. The neighbors had called the police and they'd come to his property. We were told the police didn't even try to talk to him – a 79-year-old man. A man who had served in the Air Force during the Korean Conflict. He'd served his country well as a commissioned officer and pilot assigned to the elite Strategic Air Command as a B-29 bomber pilot.

But as he'd stood on his porch, the state police had only seen his shotgun and proceeded to shoot him. One of the witnesses said, "Before they shot him, Earl knelt down on his knees with his hands in a praying position and then stood up." That's when the state police fired several shots, wounding him fatally. One shot to the head, and two to the torso. If they had taken the time to talk to him to de-escalate the situation, they would have realized he was a little confused and eccentric, but not a killer. We were devastated that Uncle Barton's life ended like this. The police report will never justify what they did to him. I knew Uncle Barton and he was an upstanding member of the community and did not deserve to leave the world this way.

After our favorite uncle's burial, we went to Granny's house on Breastwork Hill. Uncle Bart had continued to live there after Granny moved to Maple Street. I hadn't been there in years. Granny's house was much smaller than I remembered. We went inside and everything was just like Granny left it. Her furniture was still in the same place. Her recipes were still lying on the counter in the kitchen. Flour was still in the red and white tin cupboard where we used to bake. All of our childhood memories had been preserved. I had given up on having any family keepsakes, but it was like God had preserved some remnants of our past for us. We were able to collect some of her dishes, antique furniture, hand-written letters and recipes to take back home to Lexington. Those remnants from the past were priceless. I was distraught that Uncle Barton had been forced to leave us the way he did, but grateful to God for preserving memories from our past.

CHAPTER 19
MAPLE STREET REUNION

I will repay you for the years the locusts have eaten.
~ Joel 2:25a

Together we search the ashes for bits and pieces,
any fragment of our lives that may have survived.
~ Bell Hooks

Dad had been diagnosed with Parkinson's disease in 2005. It was hard watching Parkinson's slowly take away his independence - first his mobility, then his ability to communicate, and finally his ability to swallow. He got quieter and more withdrawn as the years passed, but he did not lose his sense of humor, nor his one-liners that we loved. During one of my visits, assuming he didn't know me, I asked him if he knew who I was. He replied, "If I forget you, I forget myself."

When Dad no longer could take care of himself, he insisted on going to a nursing home. He required 24-hour care that we could not provide. Even though they were divorced, Geneva had continued to send him dinner when she could. My brother, Steven, had taken care of him the best he could. Although I felt guilty and wanted to take care of him, it was a blessing in disguise for him to be given a bed in the nursing care unit at Pineville Hospital—the same place he had worked most of his life. Many of the employees he'd worked with and trained were still there.

He was surrounded by and cared for by people who not only knew him but also loved him.

In the fall of that year, I received a call from Cousin Elsie to tell us Dad's house was on fire. He hadn't lived there in over a year. To hear that our childhood home was on fire was heartbreaking. The fire department was able to put the fire out, but not before the house was completely damaged.

Michael and I went to Pineville the following day. Together we searched through the charred remains. We salvaged what was left – a few photographs and a few of Daddy's belongings. I was distraught to learn someone had recklessly set fire to our family home while drinking and smoking. Little did they know, they not only destroyed our family home, but memories left from our childhood. We eventually had to have the house torn down. When I visited Dad at the nursing home, he'd often talk about home. He loved that place. I didn't have the heart to tell him that it had been destroyed by a reckless intruder.

In August of 2007, I received a call from Pineville Hospital saying that Daddy had aspirated; his food had traveled to his lungs. I went home to talk with his doctor who informed me that Daddy was in the final stages of Parkinson's and wouldn't survive the aspiration. Diane joined me in Pineville and we were faced with the decision of whether or not to allow them to insert a feeding tube, since he could no longer eat and swallow. Dad was uncommunicative at this time. We thought it would be cruel not to feed him, although it would involve surgery, and I had promised him I would not sign for him to have surgery again. I was torn. We decided on the feeding tube.

As they prepared Dad for surgery, I explained what they were going to do. He grabbed my hand and the hand of the nurse who was working on him and he wouldn't let go. In his own way, he was trying to tell me, no, he didn't want the surgery. Here I was again making a life and death decision on Dad's behalf. He didn't have a living will, which was a mistake, so it was up to me. We decided to go ahead with the procedure but, in the end, it was not successful because Dad had a hiatal hernia. The next six weeks were the hardest I had ever experienced as we witnessed Parkinson's take Dad away from us.

In his final days, we asked Dad's doctor to move him from the nursing home to the hospital so that we could spend nights with him, but he refused, saying Dad didn't need to be moved. We could not spend the night with him in the nursing home because he had a roommate and there was no room or privacy. We added Dad's name to the list for a private room, but the waiting list was too long and his time was too short. I was frantic. Dad was a very private man and I knew he would want his last days to be private.

Since our family home had been torn down after the fire, we had no home to go to. My Cousin Drake and his wife, Serita, who lived in Tennessee, generously offered for us to stay with them, but I wanted to be as close to Dad as possible. One evening, I sat in the hospital parking lot weeping, because I had no home to go to and because Daddy was dying. My friend Teresa called just then and asked me what I was doing. I told her I was sitting in the parking lot of the hospital. She said, "Girl, you better get over here."

Teresa opened her home to me and our family during this time. She only lived a half mile from the hospital. I could see the hospital from her house and watch over Dad when I wasn't there. When I told Teresa they wouldn't move Dad, she said, "Oh yes they will. We are going to Dr. Combs' house." Dr. Combs was our high school classmate. I told her we couldn't go to her house, so we called her instead. I explained to Dr. Combs I was trying to get Dad moved to the hospital so that we could stay with him. She immediately wrote the order to have him moved to a private room. But it wasn't any ordinary private room; it was the special suite that was built for the hospital CEO when he had surgery. It was hard not to see God's hand of mercy moving on our behalf. It was as if God was repaying Dad for all his years of labor as an orderly at Pineville Hospital.

The hospital moved Dad into the special suite with sofa beds and lounge chairs for the entire family. Teresa marched into the room and demanded the nurses reorganize the room so that we would be comfortable. She was such a great source of support to our family during this time - she was our angel.

Diane and I had four uninterrupted days and nights with Daddy. That's when we had our Maple Street Reunion. Dad thought he was back at home and kept telling us to take him upstairs. It was just the three of us, as though God had suspended time for us all to be together. It was the best time we had spent together in years. At one time, the entire family was there with Dad - his daughters and granddaughters were at his bedside and although Dad was uncommunicative, he started putting our hands in each other hands. He placed my hands in my sisters' hands and my daughters' and granddaughters' in each other's hands – linking our family together. Days later, as the entire family gathered around Dad, Reverend Cornett, the pastor of Bethel, came by to pray. After his prayer, he asked, " Who in here is saved? Raise your hands." Dad's hand was the first to go up. We thought Dad was "out of it," yet here he was, bearing witness that God had saved him. Dad said very little during this time, but his gestures spoke volumes.

I practically moved in with Dad during this time. I would go home to Lexington for a few days then drive the 118 miles back to Pineville to be with him. I vowed that I would not leave him alone to die.

God, please don't let Dad die while I am gone.
I don't want him to die alone.

Daddy hung on for weeks. I am sure it was because he knew what a hard time I was having letting go. During this time, I shared with Dad everything that was on my heart. I knew he heard me because of how he looked at me. I told him how much I loved him and how blessed we were to have him as our father. I asked him to forgive me for not being a better daughter. I told him it was all right for him to rest and go to Jesus, but he knew deep down I wasn't ready to let him go. He was the last of those who'd first known and loved Diane and me. It was as if I was saying goodbye to my childhood in some way. It was like grieving Momma's death all over again. Yet, every morning I would be perched outside his room with my computer doing work. I was blessed to have my own education consulting business and could take off all the time I needed.

Staff from the hospital came by and visited with us. Two orderlies that Dad had trained came by and told stories about working with Dad. It was evident how much they looked up to him. One of his former colleagues said, "I still to this day can't get my uniform to look as crisp and white as Len's." I was able to see the impact Dad had on the staff at Pineville Hospital and to see him in a different light.

During his rounds each morning, Dr. Morgan would stop by and chat with me. He shared with me how much he looked up to and respected Dad. He said Dad had trained him to put on a cast and taught him many patient care procedures. He said, "I watched your Dad care for patients' and it inspired me to go to medical school." At one point, Dr. Morgan gently shared with me that Dad might lie there like that for weeks or even months, and that I needed to get back to my life and my family. He didn't know about the promise I had made. I vowed not to let Dad die alone.

Sitting with death is not for the faint-hearted. Watching Daddy die left me whimpering for mercy. I remember talking to our pastor during this time, he told me that death is not pretty. He said I needed to come home and let God do his work with Dad. I was not about to leave God alone with him. Yet, I called on the Lord like never before. I didn't know what to pray for.

God, please take Daddy out of his suffering.
Just take him! This is too much. I don't want
him to suffer any longer. No, God, please let him live.
I'm not ready to let him go. God, please
take me instead. This is too hard.

I thought losing Momma was the hardest thing I would ever experience in life, but watching Daddy die was the most difficult assignment yet. He was drowning in his own saliva because he could no longer swallow. I would call for the nurses to come and suction him, but I couldn't stand to watch. I knew it was time to let him go. I told him again, that it was ok for him to go and be with the Lord. I hired a friend, Abby, to sit with Dad when I went home to Lexington for respite. This went on for weeks – me telling Dad goodbye and then holding on. I remember lying there at night watching over Dad to make sure he was breathing and that he didn't slip away. I prayed, *God please don't let him die while I am asleep.* During the night, Dad would take his oxygen mask off repeatedly and I would rush to his side and put it back on - as if I and the oxygen were keeping him alive. I didn't trust God to be alone with Dad. Yet, God was the only one I could pour my heart out to.

God, this is too hard watching Daddy suffer.
Please just take him out of his misery. I don't want to let him go,
but I don't want to see him suffer any longer.

I was naïve to think God needed my permission to take Daddy. I was naïve to think that Dad was suffering when he was in the hands of his loving Father. His life and his death was and always had been in God's merciful hands. During the day, I read Dad scriptures and played gospel music for him. I would even sing to him. I remember singing to him and him rising up in the bed with a wondering look on his face that said, *"Is that you singing?"* Dad had said very little during this time. He hadn't spoken in days. He leaned up and said to me, once, "I'm all right."

I believe he was telling me it was time to let him go. Dad and I communicated more in silence during this time than we ever had through words. Maybe because of the years of experience I had reading his expressions and the things he could not say. I understood him and he understood me.

Every day was spent waiting for death to come and take Daddy away. According to Levin, "It is quite common for the dying to hold on until certain conditions are met. They may wait until loved ones arrive from distant places before they decide to let go or they may wait until the loved one who has been there day and night leaves the room." Dad hadn't spoken in weeks when our youngest daughter, April, called from Atlanta. I handed him the phone and he sat up and talked to her. To our surprise, he said, "Hello, how are you?" And then he told her to take care of herself and that he loved her. Dad never said another word after that.

On a beautiful Sunday in September, the entire family was there to visit with Daddy, including the elders, his sister Louise and his best friend Ed Pursiful. I had watched Dad go from struggling to peace. It was as if God himself was holding him in the palm of his hand. It was beautiful to watch Aunt Louise and Cousin Ed say goodbye in their own way. Watching them say farewell to Dad gave me the courage to say goodbye.

Everyone left to go and eat while I stayed with Dad. I had been to the drugstore earlier in the day and bought his favorite Dove soap and Jergen's lotion. It was just the two of us. I lovingly washed his face and gently patted the lotion on his face. I brushed his hair and told him how much I loved him. I didn't realize at the time, but I was finally letting go. I said, "Dad it's all right for you to go and be with the Lord. He is there waiting for you and so is Granny, Momma and everybody you love. We are going to be fine because God will take care of us."

My husband, children, and grandchildren came back to the room and took me by the hand and told me it was time to go home. They each said their goodbyes. I agreed to go, but secretly planned to come back in a few days. I kissed Dad one last time and told him I loved him, that I would see him soon. As I left the room, I turned one last time to see Daddy's face. He was in perfect peace.

I went back home and back to work for a few days. I was sitting at my desk in my office when my computer began mysteriously looping my saved photos across the screen. Photos of the last Christmas we spent with Dad in the nursing home started streaming across my screen. There was a picture of the two of us and also a picture of Dad with the red robe I gave him, draped around his shoulders. He had the biggest grin ever in that picture. It was as if Dad was sending me a message: "I am happy now."

Later in the day I had dinner with Michael, with secret plans to return to Pineville the next morning. I was sitting on the side of the bed talking to Michael and telling him I had let go of Dad. I said, "I am serious this time. God has given me strength to let go." Michael held me and we prayed together. It wasn't five minutes later that our telephone rang. The caller ID said Pineville Hospital. My heart raced as I reluctantly answered the telephone. This was the call I had dreaded for years. "Honey your Dad's breathing is labored and it won't be long before he goes," a nurse told me. I told her I would be there as soon as I could. I started tearing my pajamas off and putting my clothes on.

I shouldn't have left him.
I shouldn't have listened to everyone.

"Honey, you won't make it," the nurse said. "It won't be long." She assured me she would be right there with him and would call me back. I called Diane to let her know what was going on. I then prayed, *God, please take Daddy home peacefully and safely.* As soon as I finished that brief prayer my telephone rang again. The nurse said, "Honey, your Dad just passed away peacefully."

Although I had been determined to be there when Daddy passed away, I was not. He quietly slipped away while I was at home. I believe this was his last gift to me. I thanked God for the time He had given me with Dad. Time to say goodbye. Nothing was left unsaid. All that was left was love.

Part III
Life Beyond Loss

But those who hope in the Lord will renew their strength. They will soar on wings like eagles, they will run and not grow weary; they will walk and not faint.
~ Isaiah 40:31

Paul says, never disappoint yourself. Hope never lets you down. Why? Because hope is more than simple optimism for Christians, it is a constant expectation, it's a gift from the Holy Spirit, it's a miracle of renewal that never lets us down. Hope has a name,
Hope is Christ.
~ Pope Francis

CHAPTER 20
HOME-GOING

"Do not let your hearts be troubled. You believe in God; believe also in me. My Father's house has many rooms; if that were not so, would I have told you that I am going there to prepare a place for you? And if I go and prepare a place for you, I will come back and take you to be with me that you also may be where I am. You know the way to the place where I am going."
~ John 14:1-4

Death's message is one of hope and love, for it points the way to the fulfillment of life, not to its diminishment.
~ Rodney Smith

We had Dad's remains taken back to Bethel for his wake and funeral. Seeing this man who had been such a tower of strength lying there lifeless, was harder than I had anticipated. This was my Dad. I thought back to the life we'd had together on The Hill and on Maple Street. I felt so grateful that nothing was left unsaid and that God had given me time to say goodbye. It had been 36 years since Momma passed away. Momma's and Daddy's deaths seemed like bookends to my life, a clear demarcation of the past and the future; endings and beginnings. I rejoiced that Dad was no longer suffering, but my heart grieved that he was no longer with us. Diane and I picked out a sharp navy blue suit, white shirt and red tie, which was his favorite color, to bury him in. He looked so handsome.

I insisted on creating the obituary and funeral program myself. I must have typed and printed the program at least five times before I was satisfied. My friend, Teresa, laughed and said, "Girl if you don't put that program away." I was obsessed with making sure it was perfect. She didn't know that each word I typed had a memory tied to it, a memory that begged to be loosed.

Dad's funeral was fit for a king – a true home-going celebration. We invited the Jimtown Men's Gospel Chorus, who traveled from Lexington to Pineville to sing, as well as our cousin, Rhonda. Dad would have loved the music. They sang his favorite song—the same song he sang in the chorus at Bethel:

> *I'm working on a building*
> *I'm working on a building*
> *I'm working on a building*
> *For my Lord, for my Lord*

Two of his friends and former co-workers, Denny and Lester served as pallbearers. Pastor Cornett preached the sermon, "He's Ready to Go." It was true. Dad was ready to go. He had let us know as much during his last days. It was me that wasn't ready to let him go. I had been preparing for this day most of my life, ever since Momma passed when I was fourteen. I thought losing Momma would be the most difficult thing I would ever experience in my life. I wasn't prepared for the void Dad's death would leave.

We took Dad's remains to be buried at Camp Nelson National Cemetery in Nicholasville, Kentucky because in Pineville, where he'd lived all of his life, blacks were still being buried in the segregated cemetery. It was difficult, if not impossible, to find your family's graves even if you managed to make it through all the weeds and brush. The last time we had been able to visit Momma's grave was when we'd buried Aunt Dee Dee in 1994. As we sat near Dad's casket and the Marine handed me the carefully folded flag that had adorned it, it really sunk in how much this man had sacrificed for his country and for us.

Pastor Peoples conducted Dad's committal service at Camp Nelson. He spoke from John 11:21, where Martha said to Jesus, "Lord, if you had been here, my brother would not have died." I knew God was speaking directly to me. I had been secretly carrying guilt for not being there when Dad passed away. I felt like I had let him down. I had gone over and over it in my mind: If I had not left Dad, he would not have died alone. But then, even as my pastor spoke, I realized – Dad didn't die alone; he passed away in the arms of his Heavenly Father. Jesus responded to Martha in John 11:26 by saying, "And whosoever liveth and believeth in me shall never die. Believest thou this?"

I thought back to the day I had witnessed Dad getting baptized, many years ago. Then I recalled the time when the family had gathered around him in his hospital room with Reverend Cornett who'd asked, "Who in here is saved?" Dad was the first to raise his hand. He hadn't spoken or moved much in days, yet his hand shot up, witnessing to the fact that God had saved him.

Sometimes God says no to our prayers because He is sovereign and He knows what is best for us. It was not meant for me to be there with Dad when he passed away; nor was I meant to be with Momma. But my Heavenly Father had been there with both. I was reminded of Psalm 21:8, which says, "The Lord keeps watch over you as you come and go, both now and forever." I love how Matthew Henry interprets this verse:

> "He will keep thee in life and death;
> going out to thy labor in the morning
> of thy days, and coming home to thy
> rest when the evening of old age calls
> thee in. It is a protection for life. The
> Spirit, who is their Preserver and
> Comforter, shall abide with them
> forever."[12]

I was very sad after Dad passed away, but it was different this time. I was no longer that same little girl grieving the loss of a parent; I had grown up and my faith in God was more mature. I had stood at the graves of all those who were most dear to me in life and had felt God's strength and power holding me up. All that was left was gratitude for all my parents had been and done for me.

In her book, *Losing Your Parents, Finding Yourself* [13] Victoria Secunda says, "That of all the paradoxes of parental loss, maybe the most crucial is, parents have to actually die before their children can fully comprehend the totality of their influence. It is not until our parents have died – not until we can 'walk' all the way around them – that we can develop a perspective on them that permits us to begin a transformation."

Now it's just Diane and me. We are the last from the union of Momma and Daddy. She is the only surviving witness to my childhood and our life on The Hill and Maple Street. We are now part of the adult orphan club nobody wants to join. We have both survived the best we can. In the words of my sister, "The grief process is very profound, as we could only handle this pain in small doses. Imagine being twelve and your mother passes away. I don't wish this on anyone. It has truly been a complicated life. Even though – I feel blessed. Some days are still very hard. I miss Momma."

I know we will always miss Momma and wonder what life would have been like had she lived. But she left us with a beautiful gift – the gift of her faith. Going forward, we have this legacy of faith that has been passed down to us through the generations – from Uncle Bud and Dee Dee, Grandpa Jeff and Granny, and Momma and Daddy. It is a faith that has withstood the trials and disappointments of life – discrimination, mining accidents, war, and death from coal dust. It's the inherited faith that Paul reminded Timothy of in 2 Timothy 1:5: "I am reminded of your sincere faith, which first lived in your grandmother Lois and in your mother Eunice and, I am persuaded, now lives in you also." Paul was reminding Timothy of this generational faith so that he could stir up his gift. This rich family legacy of faith and confident persuasion of hope was a gift from God and first nurtured in us by Momma, Dee Dee and Granny. It is ours to stir up and convey to future generations in our family.

CHAPTER 21
BEAUTY FOR ASHES

...To comfort all who mourn, and provide for those who grieve in Zion - to bestow on them a crown of beauty instead of ashes, the oil of joy instead of mourning, and a garment of praise instead of a spirit of despair. They will be called oaks of righteousness, a planting of the Lord for the display of his splendor.
~ Isaiah 61:2b,3

Even out of unspeakable grief, beautiful things take wing.
~ A.R. Torres

After we buried Dad, we felt led by God to reunite our parents. We asked the funeral home to petition the state to allow us to bring Momma's remains to be buried with Dad's at Camp Nelson. It would be our last act of love on their behalf. Little did I know, this would give Diane and me an opportunity to finally say goodbye to Momma. We didn't remember Momma's burial, which made it even more difficult to let her go. It's strange; I remember everything about her passing – hearing the news; sitting on the front pew of Bethel at her funeral; kissing her goodbye, but I don't remember them putting her in the ground. I would sometimes dream that Momma was buried in our front yard next to the maple tree. To get through some of the tough days, I would sometimes imagine that she was on a long trip and that she would come home and everything would get back to normal. I never imagined her in a grave. What made our grief even more complicated was that she was buried in a place that we couldn't easily visit. We had not been able to take flowers to our mother's graveside.

The state approved our request and we made preparations for the funeral home to bring our dear mother to be buried with Dad. Diane and I would now be able to drive a short 30 miles to visit our parents' graveside. We carefully selected a pretty pale pink casket and adorned it with beautiful pink roses and white calla lilies. We did not have a copy of Momma's original funeral program, only her obituary, so I created a program for her service. The undertaker told me Momma's casket was still intact. Could it be that God, in His infinite wisdom, had placed a protective seal over our tender hearts and minds until we could deal with the devastating blow of losing our mother, until we could see beauty from ashes?

December 1, 2007

Death is nothing else but going home to God;
the bond of love will be unbroken for all eternity.
~ Mother Teresa

On a cold December morning, exactly 36 years to the day Momma passed away, we united her with Dad. Surrounded by family, pastor, church family and friends, we waited for them to bring Momma to the cemetery. My cousin Austin and my dearest friend, Teresa, who was extremely ill at the time and on dialysis, drove the 118 miles to be with us. If anyone understood who I had been before and after Momma's death, it was Teresa. She had been my best friend for life.

I held my breath as the hearse pulled up with Momma's remains and as the undertakers gently retrieved her casket. It was a sacred, full circle moment that bridged 36 years and a lifetime of sorrow. In those 36 years, I had not figured out how to let go of Momma without leaving her memory behind.

As we gathered around Momma's casket, I was taken aback by the beauty of the day – there was a cold, gentle breeze blowing on our cheeks and the sun was shining on our faces. As we sang,

Steal Away
Steal Away
Steal Away to Jesus
Steal Away
Steal Away home
I ain't got long to stay here
~J. W. Johnson

I could imagine Momma stealing away to Jesus those many years ago. How happy she must have been. My pastor performed the recommital service. His subject was, "She Was Precious in His Sight," taken from Isaiah 43:4, "Since you are precious and honored in my sight, and because I love you, I will give people in exchange for you." I still remember his words: "Because she was precious to God, and because she loved Him, He lovingly took her home out of her suffering." I had never thought about Momma's passing in that way. I had never considered that instead of God taking her away *from* us through his permissive will, He had lovingly met her in her suffering and accepted her in His bosom. Momma could not live any longer in her condition.

Momma was precious to God because she was His daughter and because she was a true believer. She loved the Lord, a fact that we saw demonstrated throughout her brief life. As much as we loved her, God truly did love her more. I knew the Father was speaking to us out of His infinite wisdom and in His most tender way, just as He had many times before. I could see His hand of mercy and grace, which was evidenced in other places in my life, and could understand the loving act of taking Momma home.

Momma had been right all along about God. He is loving and kind and He does answer our prayers - maybe not in the way that we want or expect, but rather, in a way that is always best for His children. Not only had I come to believe Momma about her God; more importantly, I came to believe God for myself. The last words we heard were healing balm:

For as much as it hath pleased Almighty God, in his wise Providence, to take out of this world the soul of our deceased sister Dorothy Turner on December 1, 1971, we therefore recommit her body to the ground; earth to earth, ashes to ashes, dust to dust; looking for the first resurrection in the last day in the life of the world to come, through our Lord Jesus Christ; at whose second coming in glorious majesty to judge the world, the earth and sea shall give up their dead; and the corruptible bodies of those who sleep in him shall be changed, and made like unto his own glorious body; according to the mighty working whereby He is able to subdue all things unto himself.

I'd heard these words at the gravesides of many I loved, but this time was different. With those words, peace, like a river, washed over my soul that I had not experienced since Momma passed away. It was finished. I knew it was time. Time to say goodbye to my sweet Momma. Reuniting Momma and Daddy was more than a physical act that day. It was as though God was lovingly and gently saying to us, 'Let them go. Let them rest in peace.' God was urging us to tell them goodnight with the assurance that we would see them again in the morning – "In that great getting up morning."

I understood how David must have felt when he pleaded with God to spare his child. In II Samuel 12:16-23 (NLT), David went without food and laid on the floor all night, weeping and praying for the child's life, but on the seventh day, the child died. After David learned that his child was dead, he said, "Can I bring him back again? I will go to him, but he will not return to me." All my praying and pleading hadn't kept Momma and my loved ones from passing away, but knowing that I would someday see them again, meant everything to me.

Through these accumulated losses in life, I learned that as Christians, we do not grieve as those without hope. Our hope is in Christ. Christ is our hope. I could see the beauty in that hope. Our loved ones can never return to us, but how grateful I am that we can one day go to them. This is the hope that has kept me, anchored me, and never let me give up.

I left the remains of my parents at Camp Nelson Cemetery that day, grateful for the transformation that had taken place. I left with full acceptance that it was time to let them go. They had lived their lives and they would want us to live ours. I left at peace – with my earthly father and with my Heavenly One; understanding that while God was not my Daddy, He could, and did, redeem the man who was. I was finally able to reconcile Momma's God with a God I had come to trust, lean and depend on for myself; to see Him as a loving heavenly Father who tenderly called his daughter - our Momma home out of her suffering. Our last act of love toward our parents turned out to be God's gift to us: showing His tender love toward Diane and me. As we left the cemetery that day, I looked back and saw two white butterflies dancing in the breeze.

EPILOGUE

I know the things that happen: the loss and the loneliness and the pain...But there's a mark on it now: as if Someone who knew that way Himself, because He had traveled it, had gone on before and left His sign; and all of it begins to make a little sense at last - gathered up, laughter and tears, into the life of God, with His arms around it.
~ Paul Scherer

Death has been an extraordinary teacher. At the age of fourteen, in my despair, I inquired, "What kind of God would leave two little girls motherless?" I can now answer that question. God did not leave us motherless, nor did He leave us comfortless. He is the kind of God who does not merely stand by as a witness to our suffering, but is there in the midst of it. Our lives are in the hands of a loving, caring, and merciful God. He is the kind of God who cares about our moments of grief and despair – a Savior who is acquainted with our grief. A Savior who leads us through the valley of the shadow of death. It is only a shadow because of Christ's death, burial and resurrection.

During the process of editing this book, I had a conversation with my editor and she said," God was the first to shed a tear when your dear Momma passed away." That statement went straight from her lips to my heart. As a young girl, I could not see God's hand in the midst of my suffering. I possessed a childlike faith and a tiny seed of hope – which is all I needed. As author, Donald Spoto, reminds us in his book, *In Silence: Why We Pray:*

"God does not preserve us *from* all suffering,
but He does preserve us *in* all suffering. As
for asking what kind of God allows suffering,
the only reply can be: A God who takes human
suffering with absolute gravity indeed – a God
who has entered fully into that suffering and
does not allow it the final victory; the sort of
God who completely alters the meaning of
suffering and death and provides the
mysterious means with which we can cope
with it and thus collaborate with Him in
transforming it."[14]

Alone in my bedroom after Momma's funeral, in my
solitude as a motherless child, I experienced the 'the dark
night of the soul.' Gerald May, author of *The Dark Night of
The Soul*[15] suggests that "This period of challenging distress
and obscurity when one seems to have lost everything that
had been gained and had made sense. Only a fierce
clinging to God through faith enables one to survive so
poignant time of trials." Feeling abandoned and left behind,
I clung to what I had left of Momma – her faith. Since I
didn't have Momma to cling to, I clung to Momma's God.

In the silence of the night, God made His presence
known to me in an undeniable way. He let me know He
had not abandoned me and was indeed, there. He had not
left me alone to deal with one of life's most devastating
blows. God asked me, *"Can you trust me?"* The answer is
yes. I have learned to trust and depend not only in Him,
but also on His word. The losses I experienced in my life
sent me running into the arms of God. He wanted me to
cling to Him and not my loved ones. I don't know why the
price for entering into God's sanctuary is a shattered heart.
Little did I know, my heart was, in fact, being broken open,
so God could do His healing.

Psalm 147:3 reminds us, it is God himself that "heals the brokenhearted and binds up their wounds." It is only by looking back and reviewing our lives that we can see God's providential hand at work. Dr. J. Vernon McGee reminds us: "It takes time to see His providence emerge. Looking forward, what we have is trust, and looking back we can see the results of that trust. His divine will accomplished providentially." [16] After years of bumping up against the reality of motherlessness, I began to see God's hand in it all.

To answer the question, **"What kind of God would leave two young girls motherless?"** I have come to understand that in spite of our suffering and hardships in life: **He is a perfect loving Father** who made the ultimate sacrifice for us on that old rugged cross. He died for our sins so that we can have the gift of eternal life. It is because of this sacrifice that we have the gift of eternal life. God did not leave us motherless, will see Momma again.

He is a promise giver and a promise keeper - a Father who can be trusted to keep every promise He's made to us. "So God has given both his promise and his oath. These two things are unchangeable because it is impossible for God to lie. Therefore, we who have fled to him for refuge can have great confidence as we hold to the hope that lies before us. This hope is a strong and trustworthy anchor for our souls." (Hebrew 6:18- 19a NLT). He promised never to leave me or forsake me and his promises to me are proven and true. Deuteronomy 31:18 says, "The Lord himself goes before you and will be with you; he will never leave you nor forsake you. Do not be afraid; do not be discouraged."

He is an affectionate Savior who has been a tender mother to me. He promised, "As a mother comforts her child, so will I comfort you." (Isaiah: 66:13a). As a motherless child, I cried out to God in my despair and He comforted me with His presence, He comforted me through His word and He strengthened me with His promises. He supplied me with grace, gathered me to himself with his loving kindness and comforted me as

Momma would have.

He is a refuge and a hiding place. "God is our refuge and strength, a very present help in trouble (Psalms 46:1b)." He will cover you with his feathers. He will shelter you with His wings. His faithful promises are your armor and protection (Psalm 91:4 NLT). When I felt like a motherless child and alone in the world, the Lord became my shelter and my hiding place.

He is a kind and gracious Father who gave me people for my life. He's blessed me with a double portion – two beautiful daughters and two granddaughters to love and who love me back; a kind-hearted husband who loves and supports me, whose arms have held me through the many losses; and more mother-sister-friends that I can count.

He is the kind of God that works all things together for our good (Romans 8:28); the kind of God that met our dear mother in her suffering and tenderly took her home. The kind of Father who gave me the time I needed to say goodbye to my earthly father.

It is in our suffering that God stands ready to meet us in the midst of it. All we have to do is pour our hearts out to Him. He is everything to me. He is my precious Savior, my most compassionate friend. He is My God. His arms have been my hiding place; his heart, my shelter.

As the rocks of the shore gird the sea; as the hills and mountains are round about the valleys, so shall God's everlasting arm surround and protect the feeblist soul that seeks aid. You have only to ask and trust His help in life and in death, and He will say to you in the sure word of promise and prophecy: For the mountains shall depart, and the hills be removed; but my kindness shall not depart from thee, neither shall the covenant of my peace be removed, saith the LORD that hath mercy on thee.
~Daniel March, Our Father's House

ACKNOWLEDGEMENTS

For you have been my hope, Sovereign Lord my confidence since my youth. From birth I have relied on you; you brought me forth from my mother's womb. I will ever praise you. I have become a sign to many; you are my strong refuge. My mouth is filled with your praise, declaring your splendor all day long.
~Psalm 71:5-8

Writing this book has been a long and difficult journey. A journey I could not have completed without the unwavering support and encouragement from my family, friends and publishing team. I am eternally grateful to God for planting *A Seed of Hope* in me and for His providential care over my life. It is with heartfelt gratitude that I acknowledge my support system.

With deep gratitude, I thank my family and friends:

My sister, Diane Turner Johnson, the brave one, whom I've shared life's greatest love and most devastating loss. I am grateful for your unwavering love and the unbreakable bond we share. Thank you for your graciousness in allowing me to tell our shared story though my perspective and experience.

My husband, Reverend Michael Smith, for being my number one cheerleader and encourager; for covering me in prayer and love and reminding me everyday whose I am and who I am. For being there and loving me unconditionally through it all.

My daughter, **Penny,** for the blessing of being your mother and for giving my life purpose and meaning when I could not see my way; for the beautiful way you mother your daughters and share with your parents.

My daughter, **April,** for the joy of being your mother and for teaching me to not only to love, but to live, laugh and enjoy life; for never forgetting your parents wherever you are in the world.

My granddaughter, **Candace,** for the privilege of being your grandmother, for teaching me what's really important in life and to be true to myself; for always bringing a smile to my heart.

My granddaughter, **Maya,** for the honor of being your grandmother; for teaching me to never be afraid and to pursue my dreams; for always bringing excitement and a passion for life whenever you are around.

My **Aunt Frances,** my mother's sister, for a lifetime of love and support; for being a great example of motherhood for us.

My cousin **James Drake** who has always been there; and special friends since childhood; **Mary Ellen Jefferson, Priscilla Tye, Linda Washington** and **Shirley Walker Rhodman,** for a lifetime of friendship and love.

Pastor, Dr. T.H. and Sister Delma Peoples and the Pleasant Green Baptist Church family; thank you for your unwavering Christian love and for being a 'real' family to us.

My special friends, **Geneva Turner, Saundra Bryson Bargo, Beverly Henderson, Dorothy Montgomery, Lillian Love Bell,** and **Shirley Jones.** Thank you for believing in me and for being the mother, sister, and friend I needed over the years.

A heartfelt thanks to my amazing editorial and publishing team:

Emily Wierenga, thank you for not only being my editor but for being a spiritual midwife, gently encouraging me to push through the pain when I wanted to give up. Emily, you are an angel.

Berdine Steyn & Julie Holloway, thank you for your enduring patience in helping me get my book to print and for the beautiful interior pages and formatting of *A Seed of Hope.*

A special thanks to my **Advance Readers**, my family, Starla Jimenez, Charlotte Bowling Roth, Candace Evans Peace, Cynthia Nesmith, Rev. Herbert T. Owens, Jr., Tammy Lage Covey, Lillian Bell, Jennifer Beach Fair, Mia White, and Lillian Stevens.

Each of you have helped to spread this message of hope and I am eternally grateful.

10% of the proceeds from the book will be donated to the African Children's Crusade's Ekundayo Children's Home in Kwara State, Nigeria for educational supplies and clothing.

ABOUT THE AUTHOR

Lynn Rae Turner Smith, Ph.D., MSW, CLC is an educational psychologist, social worker and certified Christian Life Coach. She is founder of Bethune Institute, School Culture Solutions, and Soulful Life Design Coaching and Retreats. She is passionate about inspiring and empowering women to discover and live in alignment with their divine purpose. She lives in Lexington, Kentucky with her husband, Reverend Michael Smith, her daughters (Penny & April) and granddaughters (Candace & Maya). For coaching and inquiries, connect with Dr. Lynn online at: www.soulfullife.org.

I would love to hear from you! Please send your comments, lessons learned, or insights about *A Seed of Hope*. Please share your own story of Hope at: drlynnsmith1@gmail.com

If you would like to provide a book review, please go to Amazon: https://www.amazon.com/Seed-Hope-Journey-through-Grief/dp/0988770717.

SOURCES

1. Edelman, Hope (1995). *Letters from Motherless Daughters: Words of Courage, Grief and Healing.* Dell Publishing.
2. Alexander, Victoria (1998). *In the Wake of Suicide: Stories of the People Left Behind.* Jossey-Bass.
3. Brueggemann, Walter (1984). *The Message of the Psalms: A Theological Commentary.* Augsburg Publishing.
4. Bishop-Becker. (2013). *Loss and Growth: The Grief Spiral: Transformative Bereavement.* Wizz Bang.
5. Chained Rock. Retrieved on July 1, 2015 from www.Kentuckytourism.com.
6. Parker, Lonnae O'Neal (2010). *Balm.* Retrieved on January 31, 2010 from www.washingtonppost.com
7. Four Mile, Bell County, KY: Mine Explosion Newspaper Stories and Death Certificates. Retrieved on March 14, 2014 from http://freepages.genealogy.rootsweb.ancestry.com/~charlottea miller/four_mile_mine_explosion_deaths.htm
8. Holman Bible Dictionary (1991). Holman Bible Publishers.
9. C.S. Lewis (2015). *A Grief Observed.* Harper Collins Publishers.
10. Smith, Harold (2003). *Grieving the Death of a Mother.* Fortress Press.
11. Levin, Stephen (2006). *Unattended Sorrow: Recovering from Loss and Reviving the Heart.* Holtzbrinck Publisher.
12. Abraham, Kenneth (1994). *The Matthew Henry Study Bible: King James Version.* World Bible Publishers: Iowa Falls, IA.
13. Secunda, Victoria (2001). *Loosing Your Parents, Finding Yourself: The Defining Turning Point of Adult Life.* Hyperion.
14. Spoto, Donald (2004). *In Silence:Why We Pray.* Penguin Books.
15. May, Gerald (2005). *Dark Night of the Soul.* Harper Collins Publisher.
16. McGee, Vernon. *More on God's Providence.* Retrieved on March 12, 2015 from http://the-end-time.blogspot.com/2013/05/ more-on-providence.html